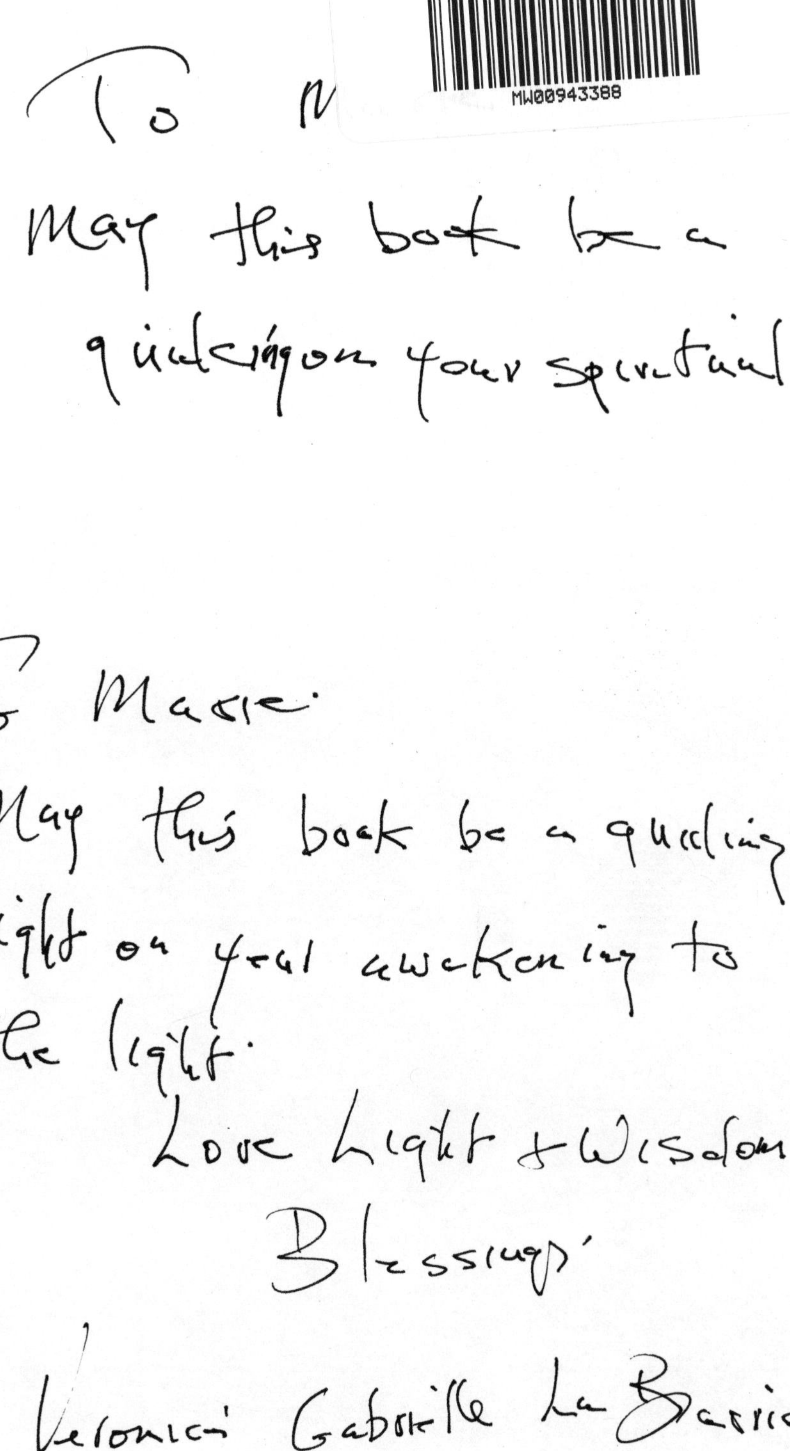

To M

May this book be a
guiding on your spiritual

To Marie.
May this book be a guiding
light on your awakening to
the light.

Love Light & Wisdom
Blessings

Veronica Gabrielle La Barrie

VERONICA GABRIELLE LA BARRIE

Ungluing the Mind

Balboa Press books may be ordered through booksellers or by contacting:

Balboa Press
A Division of Hay House
1663 Liberty Drive
Bloomington, IN 47403
www.balboapress.com
1 (877) 407-4847

Print information available on the last page.

ISBN: 978-1-5043-9831-2 (sc)
ISBN: 978-1-5043-9833-6 (hc)
ISBN: 978-1-5043-9832-9 (e)

Library of Congress Control Number: 2018902298

Balboa Press rev. date: 08/28/2018

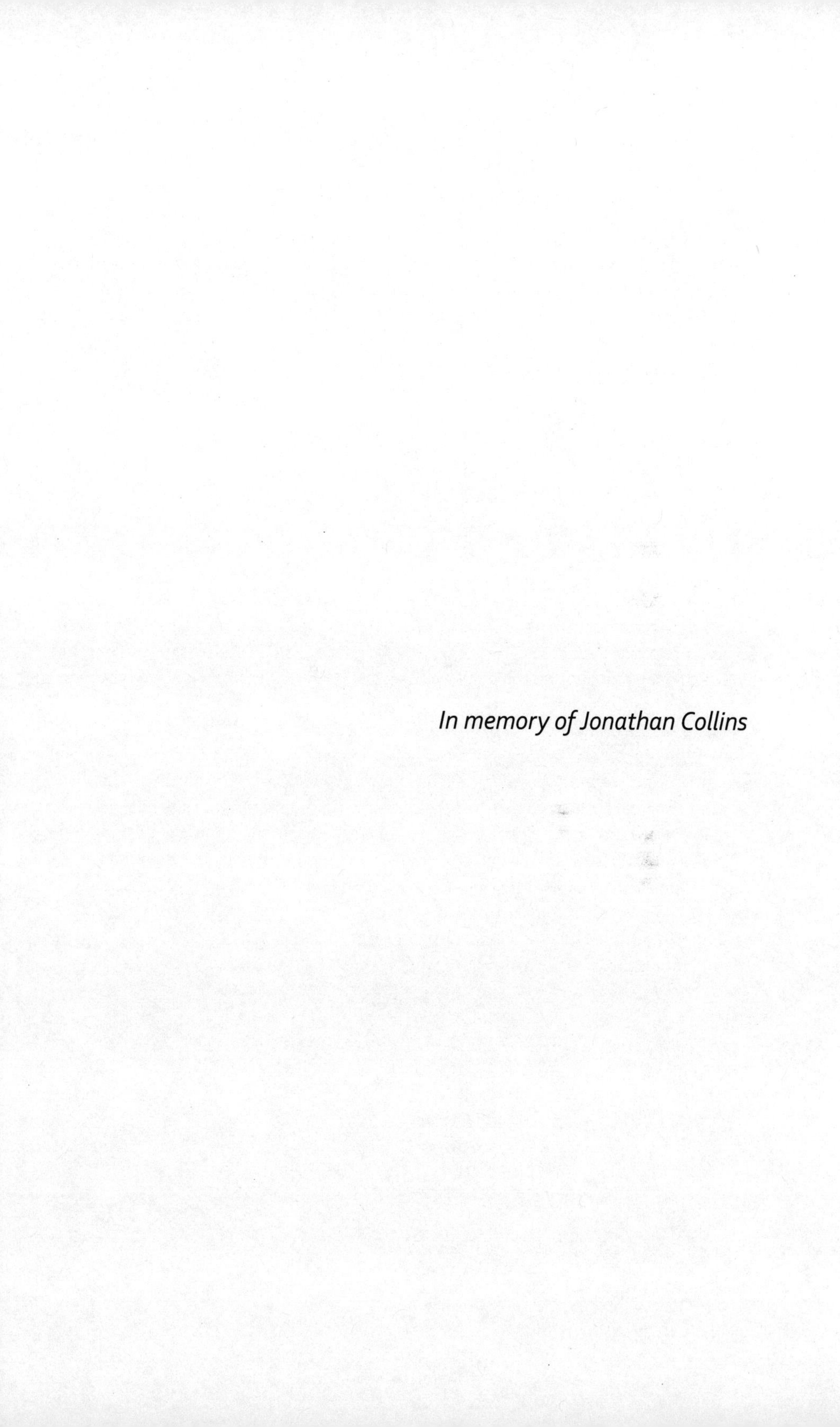

In memory of Jonathan Collins

Note from Veronica Gabrielle La Barrie: This book is intended to convey a spiritual message using an unbiased style. You will notice some passages from the Bible. They are reported in a way that shows you that its message has often been misinterpreted. It can be instead framed within a larger, Universal perspective, which is: there is an Intelligence that wants to succeed in your life, for your highest and best good, but you need to realign with it, in order for that to happen. Specific references from the Bible are found in the text, soon after the cited passages.

Some passages in *Ungluing the Mind* are inspired by specific lines from *A Course In Miracles*. I became a student of *A Course in Miracles* thirty years ago. Its message resonated with me strong and clear, and I quickly started facilitating study groups on it. Today, my teachings and writings still reflect many of the major lessons that I have learned from that powerful book.

Credits for the wisdom of *A Course In Miracles*

Acknowledgment: "Love is the way I walk in Gratitude", lesson 195, Workbook for Students, pg. 372-373 of *A Course In Miracles: Combined Volume* (3rd Edition. Temecula, CA: Foundation for Inner Peace, 2007).

Chapter 4: The sentence "simplicity is very difficult for twisted minds", as appears in the paragraph "The Happy Learner", Text, chapter 14, pg. 272 of *A Course In Miracles: Combined Volume* (3rd Edition. Temecula, CA: Foundation for Inner Peace, 2007).

Chapter 6: The sentence "He who sent me will direct me", as appears in the paragraph "Special Principles of Miracles Workers", Text, chapter 2, pg. 28 of *A Course In Miracles: Combined Volume* (3rd Edition. Temecula, CA: Foundation for Inner Peace, 2007).

Chapter 8: The question "Do you want your relationships to be host to your True Nature or hostage to your ego nature?" is inspired by a line in the section "The Invitation to Healing", Text, chapter 11, pg. 198 of *A Course In Miracles: Combined Volume* (3rd Edition. Temecula, CA: Foundation for Inner Peace, 2007).

Chapter 9: The passage "I am content to go wherever my True Self wishes, knowing that my True Self goes there with me. I do not have to worry about what to say or what to do because my True Self who sent me will direct me" is inspired by the paragraph "Special Principles of Miracles Workers", Text, chapter 2, pg. 28 of *A Course In Miracles: Combined Volume* (3rd Edition. Temecula, CA: Foundation for Inner Peace, 2007).

Chapter 9: "No one can fail who seeks to reach the truth", lesson 131, Workbook for Students, pg. 239-241 of *A Course In Miracles: Combined Volume* (3rd Edition. Temecula, CA: Foundation for Inner Peace, 2007).

Chapter 9: The phrase "Its voice will tell you where to go, what to do, whom to speak to, and what to say" is inspired by lesson 275, Workbook for Students, pg. 434 of *A Course In Miracles: Combined Volume* (3rd Edition. Temecula, CA: Foundation for Inner Peace, 2007).

Chapter 9: The statement "the Truth will set you free", is inspired by lesson 107, Workbook for Students, pg. 193-194 of *A Course In Miracles: Combined Volume* (3rd Edition. Temecula, CA: Foundation for Inner Peace, 2007).

Chapter 10: The statement "Beyond this world is a world you want" is the lesson 129, Workbook for Students, pg. 235-236 of *A Course In Miracles: Combined Volume* (3rd Edition. Temecula, CA: Foundation for Inner Peace, 2007).

Chapter 12: The statement "your part is essential to the Divine plan", is inspired by lesson 100, Workbook for Students, pg. 180-181 of *A Course In Miracles: Combined Volume* (3rd Edition. Temecula, CA: Foundation for Inner Peace, 2007).

Contents

Acknowledgement

To My Beloved Mother:

Neither happy nor sad, neither elated by praise nor discouraged by neglect, you had a secret, gentle, inner smile. You sought nothing; imitated no one. You did everything peacefully and quietly, absorbed in God and reflecting His continuous silence. You taught us always to listen to the wisdom of our soul and never to be deceived by the outer form. You taught us that silence is golden.

Thank you for the blessing that brought me into this physical manifestation.
Thank you for your wisdom, understanding, and intuitive awareness.
Thank you for being my constant companion.
Thank you for your love and the many gifts you gave. You were truly only Light and peace.
Thank you for doing everything you did kindly and effortlessly.
Thank you for your presence that breathed and radiated only love.
Thank you my Beloved Mother for the most precious gift of spiritual awareness.
Thank you for extending to me what I have extended to my children, Michael and Ashley, and all others you have sent into my life and continue to send.

May your strength, courage and perfect example continue to pilot me as I carry out my Earthly duties, so that I too may teach by example and bring others home who have wandered off and do not remember.

May I continue to do all that is before me to do with great enthusiasm, as you did. In you, I recognized at an early age what I was to become. You truly are and continue to be the Light of my world.

Love is the way. I walk in Gratitude.

Veronica Gabrielle La Barrie

Dedication

I dedicate this book to everyone in the world who has experienced deep physical or emotional suffering; to those who have lain awake at night in pain or anguish and wondered why they have been abandoned. You may be thirsting for the wisdom that is contained herein, and yet feel, when you begin reading, that the possibility of a consistently joyful, fulfilling existence is simply unrealizable. Perhaps your faith has dwindled to such an extent that you no longer hope for anything better than this "nasty, brutish, and short" life. Or perhaps you do believe there is something else, a different form of consciousness and reality, but don't believe it is in a state that is attainable for you.

Don't give up. It is the lot of most humans to go through a Dark Night of the Soul before returning to the Light, and so you are not alone in what you're experiencing. Pray, be determined, persist. You will make the breakthrough your soul is longing for, even if sometimes it appears to be a Utopian dream. Many other spiritually aware people have made this journey before you, and they can be your guides if you open yourself to them. You have to choose to open up; no one can compel you, so make that choice. Drop your ideas and opinions, and become as receptive as you can possibly be. Then a new kind of understanding will germinate within you, and you will begin your own journey of transformation.

During this often arduous journey, you will receive all the support you need. Look around you and notice the people and circumstances that are blessings in your life. Be grateful for them, and you will begin to see them in a new Light. These situations and individuals have not gathered around you randomly; they are part of a greater plan that is leading you back to the Light. When you are in pain or anguish, remember the blessings you have and this will remind you of the Light that sent them to you. However isolated you may sometimes feel you are never alone.

Ungluing the Mind is one of the many books that are here to help you. It was written to remind you of the true meaning of Life and of what you are here to do that you have forgotten. You are here to awaken from the sleep of forgetfulness and claim your Divine inheritance, in order for you to do mighty work and leave your mark upon the Earth.

The core message of this book is simple: Turn your attention on the inside, rather than the outside. Reconnect with your genuine identity and accept it for what it is: Love. Then practice the spiritual truth you learn. If you've learned for example, that no one can actually hurt you, go out into the world and live your life second to second as if that were true. Become an example for others to follow.

May this book uplift, inspire, and instruct you to make the breakthrough you have been yearning for.

Veronica Gabrielle La Barrie

About the Author

Veronica Gabrielle La Barrie was born on the island of Trinidad and Tobago, in the West Indies, the twelfth of seventeen children. She was nurtured from an early age by her mother's great love and innate wisdom. Driven by the intense sorrow and sense of loss occasioned by her mother's sudden passing, Veronica, at age 14, went deeply inward to seek to understand her True Nature and purpose in life. As a result of this, she began a process that made her discover a radically new approach to living, which freed her from all psychological and emotional stresses, unveiling a life of joy and peace.

Veronica Gabrielle's awakening has been fostered by Hinduism and Buddhism philosophies as well as by the encounter with *A Course in Miracles,* which revealed to her the key for a deep spiritual metamorphosis, moving her to become a transformational coach.

Today, the teachings of Veronica Gabrielle are mostly inspired by *A Course in Miracles,* yet they extend beyond any specific doctrine, faith or religion. Their only aim is to help you rejoice with the universal truth: You are not your separated, fragmented, uncertain self; you are a powerful, unlimited being. Veronica Gabrielle's teachings urge you to de-clutter the mind and reconnect with the Divine Source of all things. How do you do this? By letting go of your self-created, separate identity and by awakening to your True Nature, which is an expression of the Light and is one with everything.

Over the last thirty years, Veronica Gabrielle has guided hundreds of students in living a more joyful and gratifying life. And now it's your turn. The fact that you're reading this book means that you are ready to let go of everything that is limiting you and causing you to suffer. You are ready to make the shift into a new, immaculate state of consciousness. Your time has come and you need to take action now.

Unglue the Mind and be the Light of the World

Unglue The Mind

Let nothing upset you.
Let nothing frighten you.
Everything is changing.
God alone is changeless.
Patience attains the goal.
Who has God lacks nothing.
God alone fills every need.
Saint Teresa of Avila

In fifteenth-century Thailand, there was a monastery that possessed a statue of the Buddha, which, being made of plaster was apparently of little value. One day, Lightning struck the *stupa* in which the Buddha was housed, and falling masonry chipped the statue. To their amazement, the monks saw that a piece of green crystal had been exposed. They quickly removed the rest of the plaster and, when they had finished, found themselves standing face to face with an incomparably beautiful jade Buddha. Thanks to the dancing rays of Light that were emanating from the shimmering stone, the holy man appeared to smile at them, as if to say, "At last!"

This analogy represents the process of knowing yourself as you truly are. You have made the mind that now tyrannizes you. In order to become aware of your True Nature and thus live the joyful life you were meant to live, you need to peel away your self-created thoughts and reveal the priceless, eternal Mind that lies behind them. This is what it means to unglue the mind.

The Power of Allowing

No one can force you to undergo this process. Indeed, you have been successfully resisting it for a long time. But the stakes are higher now. Intense spiritual energy is impinging on you, pushing up all that you have been suppressing. Allow this evolutionary process to work within you, and the result will be nothing less than a miracle.

'Allowing' is the key, for the process is a natural one and it goes into effect the instant you give your permission. You don't have to do anything at all except welcome the transformation.

"If it's so easy, then why do I find it so hard to change?"

Because you haven't yet made an honest appraisal of your present life and realized the degree of unnecessary suffering that you tolerate and, indeed, consider normal. One of the purposes of this book is to help you do that. Of course, this will make you feel uncomfortable, because you've built a nest for yourself in the plaster mind and you're not going to give it up without experiencing fear. After all, fear is a construct of the small mind and fear is what you'll encounter when you begin to examine yourself honestly.

The Real and the Unreal

> *"But when I review my life, it really doesn't seem as bad as you're implying. I'm fortunate to live in a relatively safe and prosperous country. I have a loving family, a fulfilling job, and I experience moments of great joy. Isn't that enough? Why ask for more?"*

It may be true that, compared with others, you are fortunate. But you are just looking at the tip of the iceberg. Beneath the threshold of consciousness, you are not at peace. And the reason why is that you have lost your connection with what's real; you have separated from the Source of Being, which is the Light. You live in an unreal world of ever changing phenomena, in which possessions and people come and go. You can never be sure of anything or anyone, and, in the end, everything decays or dies. Since this occurs on a relatively slow timescale, you can forget about it. But deep down you never really do forget. A part of you knows that what you're experiencing isn't real, and this puts you into a continuous state of fear.

> *"What is real, then?"*

When you re-connect with the Light—the divine principle that powers the universe—you become the unending peace, love, certainty, and joy that you've been yearning for. These are aspects of Spirit, and there is nothing you have to do to acquire them, except let go of the 'plaster you' and allow the 'authentic you', your true nature, to shine through. Your true nature already has all those attributes.

> *"Isn't it unnatural to be continually happy? After all, bad things do happen and it would be callous to act as if nothing mattered."*

No, what's unnatural is to be anxious and miserable. Your true nature is joy itself. It is not joyful periodically—on those occasions when everything you planned and hoped for comes to fruition—but all the time. When you dissolve the self-created mind and unglue the mind, which is the universal Mind, then you experience a deep, abiding joy that never leaves you. The truth about human suffering is that however the pain may appear, the source of the suffering is an illusion.

To understand this better, imagine that you live in a world in which there is unending joy and fulfillment, a world in which there is no suffering of any kind. Now imagine yourself lying down on your bed, falling asleep, and starting to dream. You dream of a world in which there is loss and gain, love and hatred, elation and sorrow, and birth and death. Your dreams become so vivid that you forget the waking world and begin to experience your dream world as the only reality. Unfortunately, unlike when you sleep in the physical world, you don't spontaneously wake up after eight hours. Instead, you continue dreaming for as long as you believe that your dreams are real—tens, hundreds, or thousands of years; however long it take for you to pierce the illusion. This, in a nutshell, is your life.

Now, imagine that a person from the waking world is able to enter your dream world and interact with you. If you give this person, who is in fact the best friend you'll ever have, the slightest opening to communicate with you, he or she will inform you that what you're experiencing isn't real. You ask, "How can you claim that bad events are mere illusions? That's what I'd call being out of touch with reality."

Your friend replies: "I'm not living in the same world as you. Where I live, none of these things are happening."

"Where do you live?"

"I live in the Light of Wholeness. I live in the real world, whereas you're living in a dream. It's time now for you to unglue your mind and know yourself."

Opening Your Mind

The suggestion that your life is unreal might astonish you. Good, it should astonish you! What could be more amazing than the possibility (you're not being asked to accept or reject the idea, but simply to entertain the possibility) that your life is a dream? If you're not amazed, then you're making a judgment. It might be a negative judgment, "This is nonsense; of course what I see is real." Or it might be a positive judgment, "Yes, I absolutely agree with what you say; I've read at least a dozen books that express the same thing." Either say, 'positive' or 'negative', a judgment is a judgment and it will block you from maintaining the state of receptivity that is an indispensable precursor to a radical shift in consciousness.

It's important to realize that, this book operates on two levels simultaneously. First, *Ungluing the Mind* speaks to reason and imagination. It uses words and sentences that, hopefully, can be represented as images and understood by your mind. But the words also do something else; they bring you Light, which operates on the invisible, unconscious realms of your mind. This second level is by far the more important one, and it functions whether or not you consciously understand the material. In fact, it is arguably preferable that you don't understand what is written in this book! How can that be so? Because a problem arises if you start to agree or argue on the mental level. Agreement ("I know all this already") sends you to sleep argument; disagreement ("I don't believe this") closes down your receptivity. Either one inhibits the action of the Light. So as far as you can, try to suspend judgment. Not arguing doesn't mean that you accept what I propose indiscriminately; it just means that you don't reject it for now. Not agreeing is perhaps more difficult to understand: don't I want you to agree? No, because your agreement is coming from your analytic mind. When you agree in this way, you are taking the Truths presented to you and are absorbing them into your existing belief system, thus neutering them. Do you really want more of what your current beliefs have already served up to you? If you did, you probably wouldn't be reading these pages. So, try to leave your beliefs to one side and approach this book with an open mind. Don't struggle to understand. That's not the way it works; indeed, your struggle will impede true understanding.

Throughout the millennia, spiritual masters and divinely-inspired books have entered the dream world in order to tell you that you're living an illusion; that message can be summed up in one sentence, "Unglue your mind from the dream and realize that you always have been and always will be living in a state of Wholeness in which there is nothing but love."

Ungluing the Mind is one text among many that point to the Truth of our innate Wholeness and encourage us to drop the beliefs that keep us stuck in an illusory identity. Some spiritual students may take to the book like a duck to water, while others can be resistant. People make statements like, "I only trust the ancient texts that have endured through the ages." Some might find the book too complex and others too simple (because they believe they already understand the ideas it presents).

Ungluing the Mind is an expression of your True Nature. Your True Self is an energy field that is active here and now. It is not a religion, but an expression of true spiritual knowledge. The exact phrasing is unimportant; all that is important is the message. What is the message? Simply this: You are not who you think you are; wake up, and reclaim your true nature.

Though *Ungluing the Mind* draws on the language and teachings of all spiritual texts, it also invites you to look past the outer form to the universal Truth that lies behind the form and discover who you really are.

All the authentic spiritual texts, however different their origins and language, are urging you to do this. If you really understood the vital importance of their message, and its urgency, you wouldn't have time to be concerned about irrelevant distinctions. You'd want to awaken more than you'd want your next breath, and you wouldn't care what wording the message was delivered in. Your sole objective would be to see clearly that your life consists of wandering remorsefully in the past and stumbling anxiously around in the future, and your burning desire would be to return to the Light. Reality is waiting for you.

Every word in this book exhorts you to do this one thing. It doesn't matter whether the topic is relationships, money, gratitude, or even the overarching subject itself, your true nature. The purpose is to bring you back to your awakened state in which you know yourself as an expression of the Light.

Seize the Opportunity

This book was written for you. It is designed to help you make the breakthrough you've been longing for. Relax your mind, open your heart and let the words, and the energy they convey, go to work on you. A mystical marriage is taking place on this planet between

Spirit and matter, and you have been invited to the wedding. The bridegroom is now claiming the bride, for Spirit and matter are becoming one. Seize the opportunity. Join in this ceremony, in which everything you ever believed surrenders to reality and you become the embodiment of pure, unconditional Love.

Always remember: You are the Light; you are the True Self that you yearn for. It is closer to you than your heartbeat. When you find it, every question you ever asked will be answered and every doubt you ever entertained will be removed. You will penetrate into a world of absolute fulfilment and unending joy that can never be taken from you again.

Begin now to unglue the mind. Allow the Mind, which is your true nature, to appear. This is what it means to de-clutter the mind and take the pathway back to the Light. At the end of this greatest of all journeys, you'll discover that a miracle has been patiently waiting for you.

Practice

Though revealing the light of your True Self is effortless, breaking free of the illusion of separation requires effort. Therefore, at the end of each chapter in this book, you will be given some guidelines for spiritual practice.

This raises a paradox: you need to do spiritual work, and yet no technique exists that will instantly dissolve your self-created mind and convey you magically to your natural Mind. Your true nature is not in time and therefore spiritual techniques, which operate in time, cannot take you there. No method has ever been devised that can lead you infallibly to the recognition of your True Self. One of the most respected spiritual teachers of the 20th century, Jiddu Krishnamurti, when he disbanded the Order of the Star, the spiritual organization of which he was the leader, spoke those famous words, "Truth is a pathless land", he meant that there is no prescribed set of actions that will bring you to your goal. Any technique you create in order to escape from the illusion will itself be a creation of the illusion, and therefore it will push you even further into error. To express this same idea in terms of the dream metaphor, any action you take in a dream is simply more dreaming. You can even wake up in a dream, and yet still be dreaming.

So what is the purpose of spiritual practices? Their benefit is to support you in doing something that you can do even while dreaming, which is to appeal to your True Self to assist you. When you make this appeal, you have no notion of whom or what you're actually appealing to. But that doesn't matter; your sincere call for help from the invisible world is all that is needed.

Moreover, you are capable of listening to the response of your call. You do this by quieting the mind, emptying it to the best of your ability of the chaos of thoughts with which it is generally filled, and becoming receptive. The more receptive you are, the more easily your True Self can give you direction.

Finally, even though you cannot yet see what is true, you do have the ability to see what is untrue. As you quiet your mind and become present, your perception becomes clearer and you can more easily see your unloving thoughts, feelings, words, and actions. What is unloving is unreal, even though it appears to cause real suffering; as you unmask what's untrue, you prepare the ground for Truth to enter.

In these practice sections, you will be invited to repeat affirmations. Certain spiritual traditions, especially in India, have high regard for affirmations, which they call *mantras*. Other traditions view them as a form of mind-numbing repetition that sends you to sleep. In my view, affirmations are profoundly helpful. They are expressions of the Truth and carry energy of a very high vibration that can work on your psyche, helping you to excavate the negative beliefs that have become encrusted there. I recommend repeating them every day.

Everyone has personal preferences in these matters, and that is perfectly fine. Your True Self isn't sitting in the Great Library in the Sky, thumbing through arcane instruction manuals to determine whether your meditation technique meets celestial standards. The only requirements are a little of your time and a sincere intent.

You fulfill these requirements by doing some form of daily spiritual practice. You might wonder why it's necessary to do anything at all. Well, think what it means if you don't devote time to the sacred. In effect, you're saying, "I have twenty-four hours of worldly stuff to do, all of which is more important than spending a few minutes becoming acquainted with the Wholeness inside me." That's as senseless as wandering around in the desert all day and not taking even one step toward the oasis that the wise part of you knows is there, and is longing for.

Therefore, I highly recommend that at the beginning of each day you sit quietly for a while—and look within. You can use a mantra to still your mind or you can focus on your breath. If you already have a meditation practice, continue with it. If you don't have twenty minutes available (or at least think you don't) still sit quietly for a few minutes. For one thing, you're trying to establish a good habit, and for another, if you wait until the day when you have a full twenty minutes to devote to your practice, that day may be a long time coming! What's more, a few minutes of quietness will cause your mind to relax, which feels good, and, once you feel good, you might suddenly discover that you do have the full twenty minutes available after all.

Now, let's turn to the practices themselves. Here's your first set of instructions:

1) Do your daily meditation.
2) When you've finished, do your affirmation session by reading the three texts that follow. The first elicits the right state of consciousness in you, the second invokes the help of invisible forces and the third consists of the affirmations themselves.

TEXT 1 — THE SETTING

Take a deep breath, relax, and align yourself with your breathing. Listen to your breath as it flows in and out of your body. Now visualize yourself entering a pyramid. This is your secret sanctuary, and it is filled with stillness and peace. You sit down on a beautiful throne that is the perfect design for you, and perfectly comfortable. The only energies in this pyramid are your own inner energies. You are completely protected from the external world.

TEXT 2 — THE INVOCATION

I invoke the energy of all the angels, archangels and masters. I call on the violet flame to consume, dissolve and purify all my dense thoughts and emotions. I ask for the release of any tendency to be attached, for my attachments are what inhibit the flow of love and separate me from the Light.

> *The violet flame is the flame of transmutation, which consumes, dissolves and purifies any negative condition regardless of size or form.*

TEXT 3 — THE AFFIRMATIONS

- I am ungluing the mind.
- I am ungluing the mind by releasing all judgments.
- I am ungluing the mind by erasing my mental chalkboard and starting with a clean slate.
- I am ungluing the mind by allowing myself simply to be.
- I am ungluing the mind by unwinding the illusion that has surrounded me and remembering to be one with my true nature, my "I AM" presence.
- I am ungluing the mind by learning to live completely in the present, where every moment is the best, where every experience is new, fresh and alive.
- I am ungluing the mind by freeing myself from the prison of the past with its haunting memories and vain regrets, and freeing myself from the prison of the future with its tantalizing hopes and tormenting fears.
- I am ungluing the mind by letting go of doubt and fear and allowing the certainty and love of my natural mind to arise.

- All of the enormous energy formerly trapped in the past and the future flows to me here and now. I am using this energy to alleviate the suffering of those around me.
- In living for others, I come alive.
- I am being lifted up to a state of divine awareness.
- I sail through life with ease and grace, eager to serve my mighty "I AM" presence.

To accelerate your progress, choose one of the above affirmations and repeat it as often as possible during the day, like a mantra. Set the intention of making the spiritual Truth contained in the affirmation change your experience of life. For example, you might choose the second affirmation*: I am ungluing my self-created thoughts by releasing all judgments.* Set the intention of watching your judgments during the day, and when you see them, don't judge yourself for judging, but simply drop the judgments. (If you have an hourly chime on your watch, or some other mechanism that can act as a reminder, ask yourself hourly, "How am I doing with my intention?")

This, then, is the work I suggest you do. In the morning, sit in quiet contemplation and afterward recite your affirmations. During the rest of the day, practice by keeping an affirmation in mind and applying it to your experiences.

You have to be persistently vigilant. You're asleep and you're trying to wake up, but the sleeping potion you've taken is extremely potent. You must make an effort to stay awake because the habitual mind can so easily suck you back into the dream. You can be light and happy too — that's a reliable indicator of progress — but you also have to be in earnest. Pray, persist, be vigilant. This is your awakening.

The Natural Mind

Though you may experience yourself as having one mind, you actually have two. In Chapter 1, I alluded to the 'mind' and the 'Mind'. In this chapter, I'll refer to the former as your self-created mind (the source of all your troubles), and to the latter as your natural mind (the source of all your joy).

The situation becomes yet more complex when you realize that the self-created mind consists of multiple identities. Need proof? Watch yourself when part of you wants the chocolate cake and another part is trying to stick to the diet. That's two of your many sub-personalities locking horns. Because its members operate beneath the level of everyday consciousness, you're not usually aware that your life is governed by a (disorganized) committee. But nevertheless, that is what's happening.

The Remedy

So the question is, "What should I do to unglue the self-created mind and allow the natural Mind to emerge?" For an intellect obsessed with doing and getting, the answer to this question is the most revolutionary statement it will ever hear: "Nothing!" There's no need to do, get, or change anything. In fact, your best policy is to undo everything you've done, let go of everything you've acquired, and ask forgiveness from everyone you've ever tried to change. If you do this, your self-created mind will dissolve spontaneously and you'll return to your natural Mind.

The Obstacle

> *"Why is something so apparently simple, not to mention desirable, so incredibly difficult to do?"*

The reason the process is challenging is that you're so invested in the creations of your unnatural mind that surrendering them is nearly (though not, fortunately, totally) impossible.

Imaging that, early in your life, you set out on a quest to find the Philosopher's Stone. This stone is the most precious object in the universe since it can change base metals into gold, heal all sickness, and give immortality. If you could find this stone, unlimited wealth, perfect health, and eternal life would be yours. As in all treasure-hunt tales worth their salt, you have a map, which shows that the treasure is buried close to where you live, a mere three feet underground. You go to the spot, but when you reach it you do something absolutely bewildering: you erect a building on the site. And then you erect another and another and another. A wise man passes by one day, and he taps you on the shoulder and asks you what you're doing.

"Constructing buildings," you reply with a satisfied grin.

"What have you constructed so far?" The sage inquires.

"A factory, a bank, a hospital, a church, and a school."

"Why?"

You think, "What's up with all these dumb questions?" You say, "The factory provides the commodities we need, the bank managers our money, the hospital care for us when we're sick, the church cares for us when we're dying, and the school teaches our children how to live in the wonderful society we've created."

"And what's that building you're in the process of constructing, the one across from the bank?"

"That's going to be the police station. We need police to protect us from the bad men in our town who've turned into thieves. After that, we're going to build army barracks because we need protection from other cities that envy us and want to attack us."

"What will happen once you've achieved all this?"—the wise man asks.

"We'll all enjoy unlimited wealth, perfect health, and total safety."

"But isn't that what you were hoping for from the Philosopher's Stone?"

"Who needs a stone," you say, "when you can create a beautiful city like this?"

Ten years later, the wise man passes by again. "How are things going?" he says.

"Bad," you reply, "We have more poverty than wealth, more sickness than health, and more danger than security."

"What have you done about this?"—the wise man asks.

"We've built more factories, banks, police stations and army barracks, of course."

"Oh?"

Noticing a tone of skepticism in the sage's voice, you ask crisply, "Why, do you have a better idea?"

"How about returning to your original plan?"

"What was that? It's been so long, I've forgotten."

"You wanted to unearth the Philosopher's Stone in order to have health, wealth, and eternal life."

"Yes, I remember now. That was a really great plan. I'm going to renew my search for the Stone without further delay."

"Good."

"They say you're a wise man—do you have a suggestion about where to begin?"

"As a matter of fact, I do. First, you have to tear down all the buildings you've constructed, and then..."

"What! Are you insane? We've spent years creating the finest city in the world with the best services. If we tear it down, we'll have no food, no clothes, no medicine, and no protection from our enemies." The wise man goes on his way again. He'll come back sometime in the future when you're in such despair that tearing down your city doesn't seem like such a bad idea after all.

Your True Nature is the Philosopher's Stone, and, just as in the story, instead of digging down a little way to find it, you have stuck your self-created mind on top of it — a concrete jungle composed of your opinions, hopes, fears, desires, insecurities, assumptions, and so on. Seen from the outside, what you've done is, to put it bluntly, insane.

More About the Cure

> "*You say the remedy is to do nothing. But we don't know how to do nothing. So what do we do?*"

Imagine that someone complains to you that he has a headache and asks you what he should do about it. You tell him there's nothing to do, there's only something not to do. He asks you what that something is that he should not do. You reply that you've observed that he's repeatedly banging his head with a hammer, and you suggest that he'd feel better if he stopped. He informs you indignantly that he's not hitting himself. You shrug your shoulders and start walking away. He panics and grasps your sleeve. "Okay, let's hypothesize that I am creating my own headache," he reluctantly concedes, "in that case, how do I stop?" You reply, "Just stop. See what you're doing, and stop." Disappointed, the man goes off in search of someone who will give him a more satisfactory answer.

What does this analogy point to? It refers to your insistence on clinging to the self-punishing belief that you're a separate being who's compelled to wage a battle against an intrinsically hostile world. That's the painful hammer blow you inflict upon yourself. When you clearly see that you created the belief that's causing you to suffer, you'll let go of it instantly. The Truth will then become apparent: separation is an illusion; in reality, there's only the simple, eternal "I AM" presence. This presence is all power, all abundance, all life, and all love. This presence is who you are when you return to your nature.

Simplicity

Returning to the natural mind is simple. But the self-created mind doesn't appreciate the value of simplicity. It is acquisitive, and from its point of view, simplification signifies loss. It's much more interested in getting stuff. And even if it decides to simplify by offloading possessions, it compensates by taking on a huge cargo of ideas.

This is why I recommend some form of daily meditation—because when you are centered and calm you no longer feel drawn to superfluous objects, occupations, ideas, and people.

The Value of Discipline

A consistent meditation practice requires discipline, which suggests effort and thus may seem to contradict the instruction to 'do nothing'. But true discipline is a steady refusal to allow your disordered habits to continue to lead you around by the nose. Discipline helps you strip away everything extraneous so that you can move effectively and efficiently toward the full expression of your natural mind, which is the perfection buried inside you.

Discipline is the secret to successful living. As the Buddha put it, "An undisciplined mind can accomplish nothing, but a disciplined mind can accomplish all things."

Discipline means being determined to dissolve all the mental concepts you've created. Let go of all the beliefs you've heaped upon your inner treasure. Let go of everything that's unessential, for it only distracts you and delays the fulfillment of your higher power.

The Value of the Inner World

> *"So all I have to do is give up my family, sell everything I own, and enter a monastery?"*

You might be a hermit living in a cave, wearing rags, and meditating twenty hours a day, and yet your mind could be as busy as downtown Manhattan. Conversely, you might have a huge family, a billion-dollar business, and a workday that stretches from dawn to dusk and still be operating from the stillness of your natural mind. In other words, it doesn't matter how your life appears in the world of form; all that matters is the state your mind is in.

This is why mastering your thoughts and habits are essential. In the words of the Bible, "As a man thinketh in his heart, so is he." (Proverbs 23:7 KJV). This means that your world reflects your thoughts and so you should strive to keep them wholesome and pure, which is why prayer and meditation are important tools for the expansion of consciousness. They are a way of remembering your True Nature and, since you are a spark of the Divine Flame, they ultimately lead to an intimate relationship with yourself—with your natural mind. Meditation and prayer undo the structures in your mind and help you attain a state of emptiness with your natural mind. In a state of emptiness, your true being emerges.

The Nature of Love

> *"I've meditated a lot in my life, but I've never seen what I would call my true being".*

The reason is that you don't look at yourself with spiritual eyes, because you're afraid of what spiritual sight will show you, namely, love. You're afraid of love because you did not make it, and so you find it hard to accept. Instead, you accept the belief system of your unnatural mind because it's something you made.

The remedy is to demolish your own creations in favor of what your True Self has given you. But Heaven help anyone who suggests that! "What do you take me for?" you ask indignantly, "a self-destructive masochist?" Well, yes, as a matter of fact. You have misinterpreted the Divine plan, which leads you gently to eternal life, and have substituted your own plan that leads to death.

You have to suspect that you're making a mistake, and then diligently examine the illusion that underlies it. Genuine happiness, which up until now you've hardly ever experienced, arises only when you dispel all illusions and return to your natural state of mind. To heal is to make happy. It's remembering the loving thoughts of your True Nature; it's letting go of your creations and accepting the gifts given to you; it's dropping your belief in separation and, along with it, your fear.

The Nature of Healing

The decision to heal and to be healed is the first step toward recognizing what you truly want. You need healing because you do not know yourself, and therefore you don't understand what you're doing. The desire for healing is a sign that you want to know yourself as you truly are. The sincerity of your desire is shown by your willingness to relinquish those beliefs that you have so cleverly organized and developed. When you drop your self-created, separate identity, and choose to accept your rightful place as co-creator of the universe, everything you think you've created instantly disappears and is replaced by an inconceivable state of bliss.

At present, you're living an unnatural life that's being scripted and directed by an unnatural mind. *Ungluing the Mind* indicates that what you have done to hurt your mind has made it so unnatural that it does not remember what natural is; when you are told, you cannot understand it. You have taught yourself the most unnatural habit there is of not communicating with your Creator. Communication with your True Self is life.

You're either living life from the natural high of the natural mind or you're being dragged down by the self-created mind into a dark place, where the only vibration is the echo from the dungeon walls. Your True Self wants you to choose the Light, to choose life. You do this by giving up what you have made and accepting what has been given to you by your True Self, who is the principle of creativity itself. Wherever there is Light, beauty, and excellence, you're witnessing your True Self and seeing Light.

To understand this you cannot just stay on the surface of life. You have to go deep, to the root of all things. You begin this journey toward the Infinite by developing patience with yourself, by accepting yourself as you are, with all your strengths and weaknesses. Acceptance includes honesty, humility, and trust. It's the launching pad for spiritual growth because acceptance is the acknowledgment of the reality of what's happening to you right now, and spiritual growth is about expanding into reality. And healing and the expansion into reality are one and the same.

The Effortless Life

The next step of your spiritual journey is to focus on what is going on within you. What is it that you want? You know, it takes enormous energy to be negative and very little energy to be positive. When you're positive, everything flows and life is easy because you're not holding onto things or forcing them to be a certain way. You are not trying to analyze, investigate, evaluate or compare; you're just allowing life to unfold.

For the natural mind, life is an effortless business. A warm breeze lifts you up and carries you to the most breathtaking destinations, while you simply relax. You achieve this by not doing anything; not making demands or shouting instructions to your True Self. Your True Self knows your needs, and will give you anything you want, but only if your desire comes from the heart, because your True Self only understands the language of the heart.

The Power of One

> *"This sounds great, but my reality is out-of-control kids and a husband who doesn't seem to care that we're raising hooligans."*

You've heard it before, but you need to hear it over and over: Don't try to fix anyone. It's only the ego that wants you to fix others. They're already pure, whole and free; there's nothing to fix. When you're in your natural mind, you don't have relationships (in the plural) anymore; there's just the one relationship, expressing itself in myriad forms. There's no split, no separation, no isolation, and no alienation; there's only Wholeness. Whoever you meet, you're meeting yourself, and from that perspective, every encounter becomes a celebration of Wholeness. If you look with eyes of love, wherever your gaze turns you will see your True Self in everything you look upon.

The Nature of Teaching

It's not surprising children are getting into trouble. Our society doesn't know how to educate its young people. The meaning of education is to "lead out," which implies that true knowledge is already inside you and only needs to be drawn out. Unfortunately, most parents and teachers go in the opposite direction, cramming information into young minds as though they were stuffing Thanksgiving turkeys. That's how adults were taught, and so they pass it onto the next generation.

Then some other authentic spiritual text comes along and says, "Forget everything that you've learned," and people can't believe their ears. "What? Everything I went through at school or in the church was for nothing? I'm sorry, this is not for me; I'm not ready for this," and they put the book back on the shelf.

> *"Frankly, I can understand that. I've become disillusioned with religious doctrine. In fact, I*

> *don't believe any of that stuff is relevant anymore. Sometimes I think it's all been dreamed by grumpy old men who are not having fun and don't want anyone else to have any."*

Congratulations on being honest about your doubt. Doubt is a powerful tool on the spiritual path because, in its pure form, it's an energy that's trying to pierce through illusion, and it won't settle for anything less than the absolutely incontrovertible Truth. Just be careful that your doubt doesn't slip into skepticism, which is an ignorant, lazy state of mind that assumes the Truth is unknowable.

You say you're disillusioned with religious doctrine. In our terminology, authentic spiritual teachings are not a religion but a spiritual science. Religion is an add-on dreamed up by man. Its definite characteristic is that it promotes blind belief, whereas genuine teachings encourage direct experience. By this definition, a given religion may be a spiritual science, and vice versa. Names are not important; only the reality behind them is.

Regarding the issue of relevance, spiritual teachings are simply an invitation for you to know yourself as you truly are, not as you believe yourself to be. Every word you read is for you and about you. Therefore, how could anything be more relevant in your life?

As far as the origin of genuine spiritual teachings is concerned, they are not embittered ranting of a few party-poopers in the sky who are envious of your fabulous life and determined to make you feel guilty about it. The teachings reach out to you from the invisible world with the loving intention of helping you see the Truth. They want you to see that you've settled for a facsimile of the world when the real world is yours for the asking. *Ungluing the Mind* is a loving gift whose intention is to awaken you to your True Nature because you've fallen asleep and are dreaming. If you sincerely want to know who you are, why you're here on this planet, and what you're here to do, then *Ungluing the Mind* is for you. It is very profound, very direct, and very consistent, and it tells you precisely what you need to do.

The True Self

No one will ever force you to do the Work. The Truth is the Truth, however, and the sooner you align with it, the sooner you'll extricate yourself from confusion. You just have to wake up and become aware of what you know. Again, this is why you meditate, so that you can recover your natural state and remember your connection with the Source. Meditation is the vehicle that takes you on a formal visit to your true self who lives within you.

Think about the many ways in which you've tried to find salvation under the guidance of your belief-ridden mind. Did you find it? Were you happy? Did your ideas bring you peace? Let go of the illusory you that is stranded in time. Truth lies only in the present. The present is where you'll find yourself. Look there.

In your current, unnatural state, you have two conflicting evaluations of yourself in your mind, and they cannot both be true. You do not yet realize how completely different these evaluations are, because you do not understand how lofty the perception of your True Self really is. Your True Self is not deceived by anything you do, because that Self never forgets what you are. If you choose to see yourself as unloving, you can do that. But then you are condemning yourself as inadequate; you're choosing to belittle and lament your littleness. When you strive for anything in this world in the belief that it will bring you peace, you are belittling yourself and blinding yourself to your divine inheritance.

No form of littleness can ever content you. You are free to try as many forms as you wish, but all you'll be doing is delaying your homecoming. You will be content only with your natural environment, which is love. To return home, you have to relinquish the thought system that you have made. The prospect of kissing your preconceived ideas goodbye and stepping boldly out into the unknown may terrify you, but your unnatural mind is exacting a huge price from you: Nothing less than your true happiness.

Whenever you are not wholly joyous, it is because your self-created mind has reacted with a lack of love to one of your True Self's creations. If your mind perceives without love then it perceives with fear, and so it attacks or defends. When you refrain from habits that harm others, when you work to put an end to anger and separateness, you begin to align with love. Then you start to radiate joy and you draw others to you like a magnet. They are withering from lack of joy, and they're thirsting for the discovery of their True Nature.

The Power of Letting Go

> *"I've done so much of what you recommend, and yet I always seem to get more of the same old—same old."*

And here's the same old answer, but it bears endless repetition: Focus less on doing and more on not doing. Your ever-multiplying, ever-accelerating actions are a tactic for forgetting your emptiness. See that you're in a frantic race, not knowing why or against whom you're racing. When you're free from the bondage of time, you slow down, you relax, and the quality of your life improves beyond measure. All that's asked of you is that you slow down. And this you can do because you're never asked to do anything that lies outside your understanding.

So, take a deep breath and let go. That's all. Allow life to unfold as it chooses, and it will return you to your natural state of mind.

Maintaining your self-created mind, and keeping the power running to all its crazy structures, is the most tiring job in the world. Let the whole thing collapse. Then you will discover the timeless treasure you have always longed for.

Practice

Be vigilant in your practice and wholehearted. Have faith, and you will eventually develop the ability to go beyond time to the timeless realm. You are awakening to life eternal; the activation is within the heart of love, and you cannot fail. Be patient and compassionate with yourself.

Don't miss a day, even if this means sitting in quiet contemplation for only a few minutes. You're trying to train your mind and body into a new habit. Most traditions have discovered that you need to repeat an action without interruption for 30 to 40 days in order to establish a habit; therefore, I recommend that you make a commitment to meditate first thing every morning for the next 32 days. If you miss a day, start again from day one.

At the end of your meditation period, take a couple of extra minutes to do your affirmation session. You can recite only the affirmations given below or you can add the affirmations from the previous chapter.

To facilitate your work, a text of all the affirmations presented in these practice sections is available in the Appendix. When you have finished the book and become familiar with all the affirmation, you may want to adopt the habit-changing technique of reading to the complete Appendix every day for 32 days. This will represent a half-hour commitment on your part.

TEXT 1 — THE SETTING

Take a deep breath, relax, and align yourself with your breathing. Listen to your breath as it flows in and out of your body. Now visualize yourself entering a pyramid. This is your secret sanctuary, and it is filled with stillness and peace. You sit down on a beautiful throne that is the perfect design for you, and perfectly comfortable. The only energies in this pyramid are your own inner energies. You are completely protected from the external world.

TEXT 2 — THE INVOCATION

I invoke the energy of all the angels, archangels and masters. I call on the violet flame to consume, dissolve and purify all my dense thoughts and emotions. I ask for the release of any tendency to be attached, for my attachments are what inhibit the flow of love and separate me from the Light.

TEXT 3 — THE AFFIRMATIONS

- I am returning to my natural state of mind.
- I release all of my creations that block me from my True Nature.
- Everything in my life that is bitter is becoming sweet.
- I am reuniting with my Light body, melting the boundaries of my limited identity and merging with all of creation.
- I am releasing all useless pursuits and idle thoughts. Thoughts have no substance; I allow them to arise and pass away.
- I am holding my mind in silent readiness to receive the gift of love.
- Every cell of my body is vibrant and filled with Light.
- In the quiet of my natural mind, constant guiding thoughts are whispered to my soul.

Choose one of the above affirmations and repeat it as often as possible during the day. Set the intention of making the spiritual Truth contained in the affirmation change your experience of life.

Your True Nature

Let's begin this chapter by repeating the central message of *Ungluing the mind,* which is the message of all genuine spiritual teachings throughout the ages: You are not who you think you are and the world is not the way you perceive it to be.

You see separation, when in fact there is only the One. You defend against danger, when in fact there is nothing and nobody that can be defended against. You believe that your identity is something impermanent and vulnerable, when in fact your True Nature is not just powerful, but so utterly beyond the strategies of attack and defense that all ideas of strength and weakness become meaningless.

When you awaken you know yourself as an aspect of the Light. Your True Nature is love, and it is invulnerable, eternal, joyful, and all-powerful. It is waiting unwearyingly for the time when you will discover it.

"What prevents me from discovering my True Nature right now?"

Nothing! "Discovering" means removing something that obscures what you are seeking. What is that something? Your mind.

Entering the Now

"Where can your enlightened self be found?"

It resides in the "now" between two thoughts: an instant that lasts only as long as it takes to remember who you are. How long is that? No time at all, for your True Nature is not of time, but of eternity.

You do not have to look far to be in the "now"; just be willing to recognize it's within, and it will immediately free you from the bondage of time. You are given infinite opportunities to recognize this timeless moment because every single instant in your life is the now. Don't be impatient, therefore, but also don't dawdle: Why would you wait to discover your Wholeness and the power it confers on you to live a life of absolute joy, peace, love, and fulfillment forever? It's possible for you to discover your Wholeness right now. Simply drop your ideas about who you think you are, and you'll immediately see yourself as you truly are, whole and immaculate.

> *"I've read many books urging me to come into the present moment, and while reading them I feel the pressure of life lifting slightly. But, sooner or later the pressure returns, and I'm back in the same struggle again. What can I do differently?"*

You have to do the work! If you're honest with yourself, can you say you've really given it your all? If not, why not? Imagine that you've been living in a desert with only the occasional cactus to provide nourishment and shelter. A traveler, who seems unusually well-fed and content, tells you that you're going in the wrong direction. "You're heading south," he says, "but you need to turn around and go north. There you will find everything you've ever dreamed of: pools of fresh water, fruits, and vegetables growing in abundance, massive shade trees, and soft straw beds. In this place, you are never in want of anything." Is that too difficult? Head north for a mile or two and then give up when you still see only cactuses? Of course, not; you would move Heaven and Earth to find this place of unending abundance, or die trying. When you have that level of determination in your spiritual quest, you'll be on your way to discovering your timeless nature. Anything short of that and you're playing games—pretending that you want a new life but really being fiercely attached to your old ways.

The problem is that your mind, a petty tyrant currently ruling your life, knows that your liberation is the end of its existence, and so it resists the process with all its might. Though freedom from time will bring you everything your heart has ever desired, your mind doesn't want you to see this. It is terrified of the timeless moment and, because you're identified with the mind, you are terrified of it too. But how much more suffering do you want? Are you ready yet to risk everything, even your life, to see whether there's something fresh and beautiful waiting for you behind your tired old beliefs and assumptions? For thousands of years, all spiritual texts have taught you that there is something else. In other words, go into the silence within and discover that there is only Wholeness. You are that Wholeness.

The realization is the beginning and ending of all your work, for it is the answer to every question that has ever been asked or ever will be asked. To see the Truth of this, all it takes is your willingness to enter the "Now". Want that more than you want the false security and comfort of your present life, and you will receive all the help you need. Take this first step, and the next one thousand steps will be taken for you. When finally you enter the "Now", all the sacrifices you think you've made will count for nothing. As the Sufi tradition puts it, "Begin to search and dig in your own field for this pearl of eternity, and when you have found it, you will know that all which you have sold or given away is as mere as nothing as a bubble upon the water."

In the present moment, there is unimaginable beauty; nothing you have ever seen with your physical eyes comes near to such loveliness. The sacred texts tell us that when we look upon the world with purified vision, with the eyes of the heart, the smallest leaf becomes a thing of wonder, and a blade of grass a sign of Love's perfection. The present moment is a miniature of Love, sent to you from Love.

The Veil of the Senses

The problem is that because you rely on the limited information available to you through the five senses, you do not see what is truly in front of you, for the five senses are objects of mind with no relationship to Truth. Truth is whole; therefore, you cannot access it through faculties that are based on time, space, and separation. You think you are imperfect and separate, but in fact, there is nothing missing but the perception that you are perfect, whole and complete.

Your natural state is one of Wholeness; it is what you truly are. Your mind can wish to be deceived about this, but it can never actually be what it is not, any more than an eagle pretending to be a worm can actually be a worm. Your mind is pure; it is one with the Light. A mind that identifies with the physical world, and so confuses it with the body, is in the grip of a self-imposed illusion. Our intention must be to snap out of this illusion and see things as they actually are.

Shifting Perception

You may remember the time, several years ago, when three-dimensional pictures were the craze. At first, you saw nothing but a mass of dots and squiggles of little value. However, if you relaxed your focus, you received a pleasant surprise. Out of the confused, meaningless mass of color, something meaningful emerged that you never suspected was there; in one instance, which was particularly touching, a heart appeared.

It's instructive, and to be truthful, quite entertaining, to watch people struggle to see the effect. Impatient people get irritated and give up. Conscientious types try extra hard to "get it," and don't understand why the more they try the less they succeed. Inveterate disbelievers simply dismiss the whole thing as pure imagination. It seems that a person's first attempt to view the effect reveals his core attitudes toward life. In this respect, although the pictures are just for fun, they're a useful tool for the spiritual student. If you're attempting to see the effect for the first time, watch your reactions as you go through the process.

The "path" that leads to your True Nature has elements in common with the process of seeing a three-dimensional picture. The small self that grasps things or pushes them away cannot see the Wholeness that underlies all of life and without which nothing would exist. To see reality, instead of making this kind of effort, you have to do the opposite: you have to let go of control. This is frightening for the small self, whose purpose is to manipulate the apparently uncooperative (and even hostile) world so that it can feel safe and fulfilled. From this perspective, letting go is a dangerous prospect. But letting go is what you must do. Let go of the beliefs, fears, and expectations of your small self and cultivate a sincere willingness to see the Truth. Then you True Self will appear.

The Nature of Wholeness

> *"I associate Wholeness with sacred institutions, like churches, whose purpose is communication with the divine. Also, a breathtaking sight in nature can feel whole, as can a moment of profound intimacy with another human being. But I'm not sure I really have a clear picture of what is meant by the Wholeness within me."*

Your Wholeness is your Light and it is so close to you, so intrinsically who you are, that you fail to see it, just as a fish may not perceive the water that supports and nourishes it. Wholeness is the presence that resides within every living creature and every object in the universe. It is the sacred unit and Wholeness that, once recognized, offers unbounded joy to all beings.

The sacred is everywhere; you cannot be separated from it and you do not have to go anywhere to find it. Although the veils of this physical world, which obscures the Wholeness, become more translucent in certain places and people, thus allowing the sacred to be experienced more readily. You do not need to visit a cathedral, make a pilgrimage to a holy site, or sit at the feet of a guru in order to make contact with the divine. You only have to go within and recognize what is there. Imagine this: You're touching, tasting and smelling the energy from which all matter in the universe, the very stuff of creation is made. This immeasurably powerful energy has the fragrance of a rose garden whose scent permeates every room in the house. It is infused with ecstatic peacefulness and fulfillment. It is unbounded joy and wisdom. It is endless love. What you're imagining is real. It underlies everything. It is so essentially you that without it you would cease to exist. Yes, if you like, you can dream your way through an entire lifetime, mistakenly believing that the limited world you perceive with your five senses is all there is; but your dream isn't real. The fundamental, sacred reality out of which you have emerged continues to inform and guide you, whether you are consciously aware of it or not. A state of wholeness is simply the natural state of your mind.

The Power of Wholeness

Wholeness is the sole source of your power, contentment, and peace. All your fears vanish once you shift your sense of identity away from the impermanent physical body toward the Light, toward the unchanging Source of all things. In so doing, you place your trust in a spiritually pure power that raises you above the need for protection because, when you know your true identity and realize you cannot die, there is nothing left to protect. The body becomes nothing more or less than an instrument through which you express love; when it has served its purpose, you drop it and move on.

The mind is convinced that Wholeness is weakness and attack is power, but the opposite is true. Consider this: You have never handed over a problem to the small self that it has solved successfully, nor will you ever do so, whereas you have never given any problem to the Light that it has not succeeded in solving for you. Through your Wholeness, the power of your True Self is made manifest, and there is nothing the power of your True Self cannot do. Transcending every restriction of time, space, and distance, your Wholeness reverses all the laws of the world. When you see that your Wholeness is closer to you than your own blood and you understand that your Wholeness is your power, a spontaneous state of adoration and devotion arises within you. The most beautiful sights of this world, an infant learning to walk, cows grazing in a meadow, an expanse of tundra stretching to the horizon, pale in comparison with the beauty of your Wholeness.

Reclaiming Your Wholeness

> *"But I'm stuck in my mundane life a million miles away from the Wholeness of which you speak. How does an everyday person like me reach those impossible heights?"*

First, realize that Wholeness is not a far-off, unattainable state; it's so close to you that you fail to notice it. Secondly, remember that nearly every human being in history who has seen the Truth was first the victim of the great illusion that creates a life filled with suffering and confusion. Think again of the 3-D picture in your mind's eye, relax your focus and allow the hidden heart to emerge out of the formless mass of dots. In your imagination, experience the heart appearing with no effort on your part. This is the way your True Nature manifests. When you remove your gaze from the surface world, the Light within you emerges naturally.

The Power of Faith

To see what's real, you must have faith that there is something that you're not currently seeing. The universe is a mirror that reflects your beliefs and assumptions to you, and if you're sure there's nothing to see but separation and suffering, the universe will obligingly show you exactly that. Even if dozens of people around you are exclaiming, "Look at the heart within the dots", your stubbornness and pride will convince you that they're making it up. And you'll continue in this way until one day, by a gift of grace, you'll finally ask yourself sincere questions:

> *"Is there something more to life than what I know right now? Have the sacred texts throughout the ages revealed secrets that I should begin to pay attention to? Can I change myself and change my life?"*

These questions are only possible when the first buds of faith emerge in your consciousness. In fact, your True Nature cannot be seen except through faith, and the reason for this is that your True Nature is not something you know or can ever know in the time-entangled world of the five senses and the rational mind. The present moment is part of eternity, and the mind can only jump from time to the eternal through an act of faith. When you have faith, you trust in the Light's purpose even though you may not perceive what it is. Though you do not understand everything that happens to you, you trust that there is a perfect purpose behind all things.

> *"Doesn't faith essentially mean believing in something for which there's no proof? Isn't blind belief of that kind responsible for much of the world's troubles?"*

Faith is not the same as belief, and it's not blind. It is the substance of our heart's desires and the evidence of what is real but not seen. It is an unshakable inner knowing about the Truth. Though you do not see this Truth with your physical eyes, nevertheless a different kind of vision, which is slowly beginning to gain clarity within you, glimpses what's real and is ready to defy logic and reach out for it. Your beliefs, on the other hand, are illusions that keep you in bondage and limit you. You create your beliefs in order to cope with your separation from the Light and with the fear that this engenders. Beliefs change, but faith never changes, for faith is a gift of God that is eternal. It is acceptance and trust. It is a healing power that gives you the strength to plunge into the unknown.

To see an illustration of faith in action, join the tens of millions of Harry Potter fans who have witnessed Harry and his fellow students walking into platform 9¾ at London's Kings Cross train station. Platform 9¾ exists in an invisible world between platforms 9 and 10, and the only way of accessing it is to push your baggage cart in front of you and run at full speed towards the wall that separates the two platforms. That's faith!

Your current lack of faith in yourself is the only thing holding you back from the peace and joy that is your destiny. "If ye have faith as a grain of mustard seed," Jesus told his disciples, "ye shall say unto this mountain, remove hence to yonder place; and it shall remove, and nothing shall be impossible unto you." (Matthew 17:20 KJV). He meant those words literally.

Right Effort

> *"I sense the Truth of what you say, but if I'm honest I have very little faith that a miracle can take place in my life. How do I cultivate the faith that is so lacking in me?"*

Asking the question is a fine start! Pray, study, persist. Make spiritual understanding the main goal of your life. When you feel alone and afraid, you have put your faith in separation instead of Wholeness. If you have faith in your separate body, seeing it as your source of strength, then you have faith in nothing, and you must inevitably live in a state of dread, for the final destiny of what you value is decay and death. True faith, on the other hand, is the acknowledgment of your Wholeness.

You are denying your divine heritage because you do not look upon yourself with eyes of love. Yet, the thought in which you were created is Wholeness itself. When you accept your intrinsic Wholeness, you also accept the unending joy that is part of who you truly are. Surely, that's worth striving for. When you return to your True Nature, you stop interfering with Truth because you are no longer afraid of it, and so can allow it to be. Because you are whole, you can understand Wholeness. You realize that your power is infinite because nothing opposes you. Your nature is now your True Nature, and as a result, you share your Wholeness with all living things.

Practice

Be gentle with yourself. You are in a process. Don't demand instant results and then give up when you don't get them. Each time you reflect on the Truths expressed in these affirmations, you awaken that part of you that knows the Truth. In time, this part of you will become consistently present in your life. In the meanwhile, be patient and quietly confident.

TEXT 1 — THE SETTING

Take a deep breath, relax, and align yourself with your breathing. Listen to your breath as it flows in and out of your body. Now visualize yourself entering a pyramid. This is your secret sanctuary, and it is filled with stillness and peace. You sit down on a beautiful throne that is the perfect design for you, and perfectly comfortable. The only energies in this pyramid are your own inner energies. You are completely protected from the external world.

TEXT 2— THE INVOCATION

I invoke the energy of all the angels, archangels and masters. I call on the violet flame to consume, dissolve and purify all my dense thoughts and emotions. I ask for the release of any tendency to be attached, for my attachments are what inhibit the flow of love and block me from my True Nature.

TEST 3 — THE AFFIRMATIONS

- I rest in the loving arms of my True Nature, which is one with the Universe.
- Everything I need is present within me.
- I am safe because I am whole.
- I am invulnerable and eternal.
- I enjoy the outside world because I do not depend on it.
- I dwell within the Wholeness and I see the beauty in all things.
- I live from my True Nature, which is the source of my power, contentment, and peace.

Choose one of the above affirmations and repeat it as often as possible during the day. Set the intention of making the spiritual Truth contained in the affirmation change your experience of life.

Choose the Light

To discover your True Nature you need to be willing to change. Nobody will compel you; it has to be your decision. Your True Self respects your freedom and does not force its will upon yours, for the integrity of your mind is sacred. You have to choose to let go of your doubts, to know yourself completely, and to become aware of what has always been true: You are Light. You have to choose the Light.

To do this, you must be willing to give up any private, unshared thoughts and allow the pure Light to dissolve them. When you do this, in an attitude of reverence, honor, and respect, you will enter into the sacred sanctuary, where you will humbly converse with your true self and be filled with love, Truth, power, and wisdom.

> *"Can I really choose the Light? The idea seems somewhat simplistic."*

It's a fundamental spiritual principle that you have the power to choose your reality because if this were not the case you would be a victim and the universe would be cruel. The reason you don't make a choice in your favor is that you are in the grip of an illusion that tells you that what you're experiencing is your only option. Worse, the illusion convinces you that the dungeon you're currently living in is a castle; therefore, even if there were an alternative, what would be the point in looking for it?

Detecting the Error

Your initial task, therefore, is to begin to suspect that you might be making a mistake about life. You need to have your first glimpse of the fact that you inhabit a topsy-turvy world in which falsehood appears real and Truth seems unbelievable. You believe that the ephemeral world is real and that eternal bliss is a fantasy, and so you believe that a loving Creator created a life of suffering, disease, and death. You have to see what an unbelievable belief this is.

Your true life contains none of these things. It is innocent and pure, for what is created is Wholeness itself. Wholeness is present in every speck of creation, including in you, who were created in the image of Wholeness. Your mind, cleansed of mistaken beliefs, is a pure reflection of the divine and shines into the world with a miraculous power of transformation. When this understanding dawns on you, and you begin to challenge the tyranny of the belief system that has kept you enslaved all your life, then you create a true choice for yourself.

"I can't even begin to imagine this."

You can imagine, can't you, what it would be like to feel perfectly secure, tranquil, and joyful continuously? That's what you will experience when you choose to identify with the Light. Your life will become everything you ever dreamed it could be, and much more. Living in the Light, you will be a beacon of pure unconditional love that transforms everyone it touches.

The Path of Forgiveness

"I still do not understand how to get from where I am to where I say you could be."

Forgive all thoughts that oppose the Truth of your Wholeness. You can recognize these thoughts because their vibration is negative and they cause suffering. When you're feeling anxious or afraid, you're allowing thoughts that contradict the Truth of your eternal oneness to enter your mind. Forgiving these thoughts means to release them, to let them go. You are either dead or alive, and no one who lives in fear is alive. But you can transform death into life. Gaze upon the world with inner vision, as it is appointed for you to do, and everything you experience will become healed and whole. The way is perfect and the end is certain. With the Light as your support, you must succeed.

Welcoming the Light

At present, your choice not to know yourself means your mind is split, and Wholeness cannot be known by a split mind. Deciding not to know yourself is the same as banishing the Light from your mind. Fear, guilt, pain, and misery are some of the devices you use to keep the Light out, for if you were to welcome the Light into your life, everything negative would vanish, just as the night vanishes when the sun rises. The dark isn't a real entity that goes and waits somewhere until the sun stops shining; it's an illusion that disappears in the presence of the Light and cannot be found anywhere for as long as the Light shines.

Light is love. Your true environment is love, which is not divided against itself but is complete. Love is a source of nourishment and fulfillment that is inexhaustible. Remember the words of Jesus to the woman at the well, "Whosoever drinketh of this water shall thirst again, but whosoever drinketh of the water that I shall give him shall never thirst." (John 4:13-15 KJV). Drink of the waters of Truth that pour forth from the Light.

The Power of Choice

For as long as you are unwilling to welcome the Light, which means to choose your True Nature, you will remain divided, with the result that you will remain in pain and suffering. All suffering is some form of external searching because all that you ever find outside of you is impermanence, decay, and death. What you fail to realize is that you're choosing to identify with and put your faith in external temporary phenomena; you're choosing suffering.

> *"But I don't choose suffering. When I get sick, or my business doesn't go well, do you expect me to believe that I choose these events or the suffering that accompanies them?"*

Actually, you do choose these events, because the universe operates according to the law of attraction. So if you believe in disaster, you'll get disaster, not as a punishment — only the split mind, which doesn't know the Truth about itself, entertains the concept of punishment — but as an inevitable consequence of what you choose to believe. You don't choose the suffering directly, but you do choose it indirectly by being a host to negative thoughts that attract negative conditions.

Sickness is also a decision, not an accident, whose secret purpose is to hide reality. You have concluded that you are your body, and when you get sick and are in pain you confirm your identification with the body and thus confirm what you have concluded. In this way, you persist in hiding the Truth from yourself, which is that you are not the body. By being sick, you demonstrate that you can be hurt and that you need external help. If you were to turn around and confront this illusion, you would come face to face with one of your greatest fears, the fear of awakening. You continue to identify with your impermanent body because you are afraid of knowing your true essence.

> *"But this doesn't seem true. In fact, I'd say the opposite is the case: negative thoughts choose me and, whatever I do, I can't seem to get rid of them. And sickness just happens to me; I'd like to choose health, but I can't."*

Life seems this way because you created the illusion that enthralls you, and so you have an unshakeable belief in it. You think you are a separate individual living in a universe that "does things to you." This belief causes you to feel like a victim because you don't think you have any control over what happens. It's as though you decided to wear a blindfold and then started to blame chairs, trees, and other people for bumping into you. The solution should be simple (take the blindfold off and allow Light to come to you), but the difficulty is that you've forgotten that you're wearing a blindfold.

The Power of Presence

The solution to this difficulty is to look within. Decide that you will withdraw your gaze from the external, impermanent world and will instead look inward to find your Wholeness that can remove all pain, end all sorrow, and solve all problems. When difficulties of any kind arise, apply the power of presence to them, and challenge the fear that has kept you enslaved all your life. Fear flourishes in a mind that is obsessed with the past and future, but it has no existence in a mind that is present.

Because everything in time changes, a mind in time is a mind living in a nightmare. A still mind, on the other hand, is at peace because your True Nature does not change. Your rebirth into the present moment is your salvation from the identification with impermanent phenomena, that causes you to suffer. Stop defending yourself from your experiences. There is nothing that needs defending. The simple Truth is that defenses are plans to protect what cannot be attacked. The more defenses you have, the more you reinforce the false idea of your vulnerability, and the more insecure you become. Be defenseless because therein lies your safety.

Defensiveness is weakness, whereas defenselessness is strength because, when you are whole, nothing opposes you and thus no defense is needed. Your True Nature, therefore, is your strength. Seeking answers from your small self has never provided a true answer to anything, and it never will, because it isn't who you truly are. Choose differently. Look within and favor Truth over illusion, strength over weakness, and mastery over slavery.

A Case of Mistaken Identity

Another way of describing the problem is that you've made a mistake about who you are. The spiritual teacher Gurdjieff used to explain this with the analogy of a horse and carriage. He told his students, "Imagine what would happen if you thought you were the horse and allowed it to take charge: you would go places, but only rarely (and then by pure chance) would you arrive somewhere that was meaningful and inspired by higher understanding. Your journey would be one disaster after another. Now imagine that you break the spell that has made you give your power over to the horse. You become aware of yourself sitting in the carriage; you remember how to direct the horse so that it is your servant, not your master; and your journey now takes you to the destination determined by your human consciousness. You return to a proper relationship with your horse, which instead of being a liability to you—now becomes a useful ally."

The self-created mind, the ego, does not know where it is going; it is an expert only in confusion. It cannot give you anything because it does not exist independently of you. It is essentially nothing, and being nothing, it has nothing to offer. It is trying to teach you who you are without truly knowing who you are. Imagine you have written and directed a movie in which your country is at war and your home is being attacked. There's nothing wrong with this unless you forget that it's a movie of your own creation. When you think it's real and erect defenses around your home in fear of an imminent assault, then, viewed from the outside, your behavior appears insane.

You have a choice: To listen to madness or to hear the Truth. Although simplicity is very difficult for twisted minds, Truth is simple. It is clear and easily understood. The Truth of who you are will be immediately apparent if you sincerely want to know it.

"I feel I've sincerely wanted to know the Truth, but perhaps I've been deluding myself."

Having the honesty to acknowledge this is vital. See that you haven't been totally sincere and become genuinely devoted to the re-discovery of your true identity. Pray for guidance, but do so with a humble, sincere heart. Your small self cannot help you in this way because it is divided. You cannot ask the Light for anything from a divided mind because, when you are split, you cannot communicate meaningfully or receive the full impact of an experience; and so you are always left feeling empty. This emptiness compels you to seek more experience in order to fill the void, but you never succeed in doing so, and the result is disappointment and disillusionment.

The sense of never having enough arises from our mistaken identity. Who you really are is a manifestation not of lack, but of endless fulfillment. Look within, toward that part of you that authentically longs for the Truth; it will guide you and will help you see that the Light is not something you bring about, but something that has always existed and always will exist. When you realize this, you will no longer pry or yearn, since you do not have to pry or yearn for what you already have.

The Relief of Letting Go

When you rediscover your True Self, you can relax. You are not in control of outcomes, and that is just fine with you. You've spent your life trying to get the results you want and all you've managed to obtain is more anxiety and more insecurity. What a relief to hand the reins over to an intelligence that knows how to guide you. You can finally work and play without tension because you are not anxious or excited about the results. Your true self does not insist on getting its own way; being aware of itself and its connection with the Light, it lets the Light take charge and it watches in joyful gratitude as a life of miracles unfolds.

Heaven is here and now. You are here to live Heaven on Earth, which means living from your authentic self, doing what you love, and loving what you do with passion.

> *"Heaven on Earth? Is that possible? Only a handful of men and women in history have supposedly experienced the Truth of this."*

Yes, in the past, few people in any generation discovered the Truth of who they were; but the world is changing rapidly and what is true then is not true now. Do not let the past dictate to you how the present must be. Just because a thing has often been so, doesn't mean it must always be so. Listen to your internal voice and refuse to let external information direct your life.

Listen from within and know your True Self. Your Wholeness is certain, and certainty is of your True Self. In letting go of small self-attachments, you are not losing anything except uncertainty and skepticism. What you discover when you stop seeking safety outside is that you have an inner strength that cannot be broken.

A Smidgeon of Determination

Look within and find the Truth about this. You cannot be casual about your search. Casualness creates casualties. To soar high in the sky of Wholeness requires a simple, pure, courageous heart. Take the first step, and you will be helped. You have not been abandoned; expel the word from your vocabulary. As soon as you set your intention in the right direction, all manner of assistance will come to you. Like a ship, you are made for sailing, not for sitting in the harbor. Make the effort to get out into open water, and divine winds will arise and propel you safely onwards. Do you want to sit in the harbor and talk about sailing, or do you want to go on a voyage that leads you to your destiny? Do you want to think about the Light, or do you want to be the Light?

"Tell me more about what I need to do in order to make a breakthrough. How do I choose the path of Light and not the path of darkness?"

You choose the path of Light when you devote time to studying spiritual teachings or some other authentic expression of Truth. Emanations of the sacred, the teachings bring you to the awareness of your Wholeness, to the actual state of recognizing your True Self. They lead you step by step, through a process in which you awaken from the dream of separation and experience the reality of Wholeness. When you study sacred writings, you are a co-creator, working with the Light to transfer your place of residence to your native home. Remember, however, that the teachings are not to be learned, they are to be lived. Ultimately, even the teachings will have to be dropped, once you transcend all concepts and enter into a living experience of Truth. You'll know you're still stuck in concepts if, when life throws up another challenge, as it will inevitably do, all your spiritual knowledge abandons you and you have no clue how to respond. Don't despair when that happens; use the information to move back into your living, spontaneous, True Self. It always knows how to respond, whatever happens in the external world.

Don't be discouraged or allow appearances to obstruct your inner vision. You are enlightened because your mind is part of the universal Mind, and since you are whole, your sight must also be whole. Your sight is related to your True Self, not to your ego. Your purpose is to see the world through your own inner eyes that are illumined by the Light. Remain rooted and do not project the beliefs of your self-created mind onto the world. When you are taken over by negative thinking and painful feelings, try to remember that you're trapped in a self-perpetuating illusion. Pray, persist, be determined, and be vigilant. Become aware that the mind's judgments give you false direction, and make contact with the inner vision that shows you what is true and where to go. Your inner vision shows you Wholeness and, because Wholeness is real, it shows you the Truth. Truth cannot be invented; it can only be recognized. Your task is to recognize what is already there and choose it. See that the way you have been living has not brought you joy. Admit that you are disillusioned. Ask yourself whether there might be another approach to life, one that is purposeful and fulfilling. Be curious about your True Self, about who you truly are. At present, you are swimming in treacherous waters in a storm.

Be honest about the fact that your strategies so far have failed to guide you into a place of lasting calm, and drop those strategies. A colleague, for example, takes credit for your work? Well, you've tried being angry, judgmental and indignant a thousand times and all it's done is put you into an angry, judgmental and indignant state. Do you really want to experience that again? Do you really want to continue believing the voice that tells you that you must retaliate? Retaliation is the harm you're trying to avoid. Practice the new strategy of total acceptance, and observe what happens.

Embracing All Experiences

When you choose the Light, you welcome events and do not judge them. All judgment is suspended since judgment is of time. Your mind believes that without judgment it would be overwhelmed by the world and lived in chaos, for judgment is its way of making sense of phenomena and then acting to avoid or acquire what it sees. But, in fact, without judgment all is Love, for Love is perfect acceptance, the recognition that all minds are joined, and that nothing needs changing. Since Wholeness is union with your True Self, there is no conflict with your True Self for all needs are unified in the Divine Mind. In the present moment, there is no need except one: To share love.

> *"But if I accept everything and judge nothing, doesn't that mean everyone will walk all over me?"*

Acceptance isn't passivity; it's the state out of which intelligent action can arise. Contemplate the words of the Chinese sage, Seng-Ts'an, "The Perfect Way is only difficult for those who pick and choose. Do not like, do not dislike; all will then be clear. Make a hairbreadth difference, and Heaven and Earth are set apart."

Acceptance is the first step of the journey back to your True Self. Be one-minded, for the completion of this journey requires your undivided decision to return to your True Self. Uproot, therefore, all your shallow thoughts; otherwise, they will lead you astray.

You are Rich in Spirit

Remember that life is not about getting, but about giving: You do not have to get love and Wholeness, for they are gifts that you were born with. When you recognize this Truth, you begin to live from your True Self, and then giving is natural to you, because unconditional giving is one of the attributes of your True Self, who is the source of your Wholeness. Realize that you are already whole, inspired, and spiritually rich. Your wealth has nothing to do with material possessions. Your only real poverty is to be poor in spirit, and just as your only real self is to be rich in spirit. Richness of spirit means that your thoughts are wholesome and pure, that you are rich in the richness of your True Self. You have nothing to learn and nothing to obtain. You have awakened to your True Self in which you are connected to the eternal source of life, where your beliefs in separation are replaced with the knowledge of Wholeness. In this place of spiritual richness, you abide in joy.

Be still and know that your True Self will be secure in this knowledge, and will effortlessly live in absolute freedom. Choose to dwell in the infinitely rich silence. Choose the Light, which is perfect fulfillment. Choose Heaven on Earth.

Practice

1) Do your daily Meditation.
2) At the end of your meditation period, begin your affirmation session.

TEXT 1 — THE SETTING

Take a deep breath, relax, and align yourself with your breathing. Listen to your breath as it flows in and out of your body. Now visualize yourself entering a pyramid. This is your secret sanctuary, and it is filled with stillness and peace. You sit down on a beautiful throne that is the perfect design for you, and perfectly comfortable. The only energies in this pyramid are your own inner energies. You are completely protected from the external world.

TEXT 2 — THE INVOCATION

I invoke the energy of all the angels, archangels and masters. I call on the violet flame to consume, dissolve and purify all my dense thoughts and emotions. I ask for the release of any tendency to be attached, for my attachments are what inhibit the flower of love and separate me from my True Self.

TEXT 3—THE AFFIRMATIONS

- I choose Light.
- I am releasing all that I've been holding onto for security and satisfaction.
- Regardless of my perception, I know that I am being transformed and that all is well.
- I am gentle with myself. I accept myself and I am kind to myself.
- I am content in every moment.
- I am reuniting with my Light body and with the awareness that I have lost.
- I am grateful for this day; whatever transpires I face with love and understanding.

- I perform every task with a grateful attitude, thankful that I can be used.
- The channel is open and I put myself in the service of the Light.

Choose one of the above affirmations and repeat it as often as possible during the day. Set the intention of making the spiritual Truth contained in the affirmation change your experience of life.

Walking the Path of Gratitude

Gratitude is a healing flower that blossoms in our hearts as we unglue the mind by releasing hopes, fears, and expectations and by opening ourselves to the Light. Gratitude reveals to us the beauty and perfection of Creation and guides us into a state of continuous joy and wonderment. It corrects the error that makes us believe we live in a hurtful world that must be defended against and controlled and shows us instead that goodness and love animate every event and experience, no matter how big or small, whether it be the birth of a universe or the formation of a snowflake. Gratitude does not grow alone, for, wherever it blooms, rooted nearby in the same soil of the heart, the flowers of perfect love, peace, and Wholeness are always found.

Spiritual Sight

> *"I know I should be grateful for all I have because compared with many other people in the world I have a lot. But, frankly, I find it hard not to be depressed about my life the way it is now."*

The reason you experience so little gratitude in your life is that you look at the world through your body's eyes and fail to see the true value there. Because you identify with your body, what you see is a world that intends to destroy you, instead of an ever-flowing life force that loves you. It's as if you were strolling by the ocean and saw a bleached jellyfish; knowing its sting can be dangerous, you give it a wide berth, and in doing so you pass by this translucent miracle of the sea and remain entirely unaware of the gifts it has to offer you. Multiply this example by hundreds of instances a day in which the mind, in its frantic attempt to control a hostile reality, wraps you in a fog that blinds you to reality, and the end result is your life as you now know it. Without spiritual sight, you're not present and you miss the beauty that's right in front of you. You're mourning the past or projecting into the future, and you don't see what's truly here now. Whatever the circumstances of your external life, in the now there is only joy and infinite love.

Mistakenly believing you are your body, you in effect believe that you are separate from your True Self. This gives rise to fears, doubts, and conflicts. In the world as a whole, it gives rise to war, economic hardship, broken families, unenlightened education, environmental devastation, and a proliferation of increasingly insane laws. But in Truth, you can no more be disconnected from your True Self than dayLight can be disconnected from the sun. However, the belief that this is so, makes you forget your true home and take up residence in the fragile, impermanent mechanism known as the body. This mistake is at the root of all your suffering.

> *"But I do live in my body. I don't see how this is a mistake."*

Yes, you have a body, but there is so much more to you than that. Once you see your True Self through the eyes of Spirit, you remember who you are. Then everything you see outwardly changes, and gratitude becomes your natural state.

Your Mansion on the Hill

Imagine that you were born in a mansion on a hill. In this mansion, there is everything you need; you have only to think of it and it is brought to you. Outside, the magnificent gardens are full of trees laden with magical fruit that quenches your hunger more completely than any food you have ever known. Whenever you choose to pay attention to it, you notice tranquil music playing, and the fragrance of rose petals fills the air at your inner mental command. Everything unfolds according to the deepest desires of your heart. But as a young child, you wandered down to the part of the property where the swamp is, and you forgot about the mansions. By the swamp there's a cabin, and what a dilapidated structure it is. The boards are rotten, the roof is leaking, the door lets in the rain but fails to keep out rodents (not to mention the alligators that waddle out of the muddy waters a night and keep you in a state of perpetual terror). It's a miserable existence, spent fixing the cabin, defending against the weather and the dangerous animals, and foraging for scraps of food that never seem to satisfy you.

From time to time, you are given hints suggesting that you are making a huge mistake. You read about it in books. And if you're fortunate, someone who lives in a mansion may visit you. They tell you about your error and, though you sense there's something different about them, you laugh and say, "The mansion sounds deLightful, but right now I need some help fixing the leak in my hut. Perhaps you could fend off the alligators while I work to plug the holes". The sad part is that you keep on fixing and plugging, sometimes your whole life through, but nothing you do ever turns your cabin into a mansion. The only solution is to turn your gaze away from your temporary hovel by the swamp and start to glimpse the permanent palace that's waiting on the hill for your return.

In real life, the hut is your impermanent, physical being and the mansion is your True Self. While you live in the hut, you succumb to the illusion that your experiences are sometimes good and sometimes bad. You operate from the premise that the world is threatening, which causes you to try to manipulate the present and control the future according to your interpretation of the past. Letting go and allowing life to unfold according to its own inherent design thus seems a foolhardy option, when in fact it is your freedom.

More on Forgiveness

Letting go is the true meaning of forgiveness. Give up your illusions so that there is space in your mind for what is real; when you do this, you understand that what seemed negative was in fact always a gift to you, with no exceptions. The experience that flows from this state of understanding is one of gratitude, which then acts to release you from the past and return you to the present, where you can see the inestimable value of all things. The future clears up automatically when the past is understood without error because your reaction to the future is determined by your mistaken beliefs about the past. The future is imaginary thought projection — this is what I want to do, this is what I need to have, and so on. In this state of mind, you overlook the present and are unable to be grateful for what's in front of you right now.

More on Spiritual Sight

In order to experience gratitude, therefore, see every instant of life as a gift. Instead of insisting on looking outward with the body's eyes, gaze inward, using spiritual sight, and access the Wholeness that is already within you. Whatever you do when you look through the body's eyes just encourages your mind to interpret life as a series of problems to be solved, and causes you to keep repeating the same error in a different form, trying to fix the problem. But problems are not caused by anything that happened in the past; they arise because you constantly weigh down the immaculate present with your mind's fearful interpretations of the past, which only leads to more and more mess. The Truth is: Nothing is happening outside. Every event is in itself neutral, serving only one purpose, to guide you back to your true home in the Light. Your perception of events as pleasing or threatening is the consequence of a story that you create inside the mind. In Shakespeare's words, "There's nothing good or ill, but thinking makes it so." Everything is arising in the mind. That's where the error was first made, and so that is where the correction must take place.

The One and Only Problem

> *"I have so many problems it would take more than a lifetime to clear them all up!"*

However, it might appear to the self-created mind, you have only one problem, which is a result of only one error, and thus requires only one solution. There are no big or little problems, there's only the one problem of your belief in separation from the Light. The fact is you've shut the door on your True Self, and there is only one solution to that: Open the door again and reconnect with your True Self.

Dropping Judgments

> *"How do I reconnect with my True Self?"*

To begin the process, and to access the gratitude that will ultimately both heal you and be a consequence of your healing, you have to stop your mind from judging your experience. You perceive events as good or bad, but they are simply what they are, nothing more. When you judge what happens, you lack true understanding. On the other hand, if you accept without judgment what is, then you know exactly what is needed in any situation. Judgment creates negativity and blocks the flow of energy, which leaves you confused and uncertain about what to do. But if you drop your judgments, you can access the wisdom that's already inside you.

Ask, "What can I do in this situation; how can I be of service?" and guidance will come, for your determination to live without judgment is an invitation to the Light to enter your life. The Light has been waiting for this moment when finally it can lead you, in ways appointed for your happiness according to the ancient plan, begun when time was born. Everything that's happened in the memory traces of your mind has been an opportunity for you to go more deeply within yourself. When you glimpse the Truth of this, gratitude gradually flowers within you and begins its work of releasing your mind from the past. For as long as you're busy judging your past experiences, you remain stuck because you're unable to let go and experience the freshness of the now moment as it really is.

Your judgments are like glasses with thick lenses that distort everything you see. Once you stop complaining about the outer world and simply take off your judgment-created lenses, for the first time you see things as they are. Gratitude serves to correct your perception; it is a healing balm that gently moves you into the present.

The practice of gratitude, therefore, is a technique for correcting your error. It dissolves your tendency to fight life and feeds a new attitude in which you learn to accept exactly where you are and what's going on right here and now. It shows you how to see and use every experience as an opportunity for correction.

The Power of Your Will

But first, you have to be willing to do this, for nothing is ever forced upon you. You have to be willing to recognize that life is continually offering you an opportunity to let go of your old beliefs. You have to welcome a change in your mindset and allow the error to be corrected. You have to be tired of forever reacting out of your state of fear and instead devoutly wish to live in a new way that is characterized by a state of gratitude and love.

Authenticity

> *"I'm making an effort to be grateful for everything that happens, as you recommend, but to be honest I don't feel authentic about it. I say, 'Oh, this calamity is happening for the best and ultimately everything*

will turn out well', but the calamity still feels like a calamity."

What's happening right now is a tragedy, you tell yourself, but good will come from it in the end, and so all will be well. No! Though this thinking is a form of optimism, it's still the error of a divided mind. To the awakened mind, there's no such thing as a bad circumstance or event. The perception of a bad thing results from lack of awareness; the so-called negative experience is actually an opportunity to regain awareness, and therefore it's a gift. If you perceive reality correctly, you can feel grateful for events that seem tragic, not because you trust that in the future they will change for the better, but because you see the loving gift that is being offered to you right here and now.

Another Look at Time

All negativity arises from resistance to the now. You believe you cannot function without time and that you have to manipulate the future according to what you've learned from the past. However, time is an illusion. The body is in time but your True Self is beyond time; it is eternal.

Another Look at Identity

When you persist in identifying with the body, you cannot help but feel compelled to defend it. This requires creating plans in time in order to protect yourself from the threatening world, even though it is you, yourself, who created the threat in the first place. You did this by forgetting your True Self and identifying yourself with something impermanent. How can identification with something that dies have any other result than suffering and fear? When you make this mistake, you become preoccupied with time, because you take yourself to be something vulnerable and then have to create defenses to protect it. All the problems you have in your individual life, and all the problems that afflict communities and nations, stem from this paradigm.

You don't need to have any problems in your life. Problems are not what your True Self has planned for you; if you realized this, you would view your life very differently. What could you not accept, if you but knew that everything that happens, all events, past, present and to come, are gently planned by your True Self whose only purpose is your good? If you could see with spiritual sight your True Self's infinite bounty, you would naturally be grateful. But since your mind is no longer in its natural state of Wholeness, and you're lost in an illusory world of your own making, you cannot see the astonishing beauty of every instant of your life. Pure gratitude is therefore impossible for you.

True Value

You don't see life as it is or experience true gratitude because your beliefs dull your mind and distort your perception. You fail to distinguish the valuable from the worthless, and so you don't see what there is to be grateful for. A person can stumble upon a chest of Spanish gold coins, but if all he sees is a disappointing pile of useless metal, he will pass it by. In its natural state, unencumbered by resentments from the past and fears of the future, the mind is present, and in that state of presence, it sees everything as a gift.

The Illusion of Tomorrow

"Again, the usual question: How can I bring this about?"

Are you ready to see a different reality and bring about a transformation? Do you truly want to take responsibility, or do you unconsciously want to keep playing the game in which you talk casually about change without ever truly changing? Are you putting off until later what can be achieved only now? Are you reading this book today, for example, so that you can know the Truth tomorrow? You need to realize that this future, in which you invest so heavily, has nothing for you. Your real thoughts, which are what you really seek, are not in the future, but in the present; the now moment is the only place in which you'll hear them. In the now, every experience you have is new, fresh and alive. In this state of Wholeness, you are spontaneously grateful.

Connection to the Source

A mind in a state of Wholeness is a mind in a state of constant gratitude because being fully in the present moment, where there is only love, it sees the infinite value of all things, and their goodness. Constant gratitude is the automatic expression of a mind that has returned to its natural state, which means being consciously connected to the Source.

The mind achieves this conscious connection by letting go of its error. There is nothing for the mind to get; only something for it to lose. Thinking there is something to get makes no sense to the True Self because it sees the impossibility of not being what it is. Thus, the mind has to reverse its usual pattern of seeking to acquire something, and instead, let go, and allow the True Self to take charge.

Even if you don't easily feel your connection with Source, and so fail to experience the natural flow of appreciation for life, practice gratitude diligently and you will change, for gratitude is the healing agent of the soul that lifts you out of any condition of negativity or lack. The greatest of all attributes, it is an alchemical energy that transforms insanity into sanity. It goes hand in hand with love, for where one is, the other is also found. Gratitude paves the path that leads to your sacred self and accelerates your journey home.

> *"So an attitude of gratitude brings me into the present moment?"*

Exactly! You cannot be regretful about the past and fearful about the future and experience a true state of gratitude. Therefore, your intention to be grateful has the effect of returning you to the now moment, to your "I AM" presence, to your True Self. In the present moment, you drop your time-forged plans and allow Life to unfold effortlessly. If there is an action to take, it will be shown to you. If there is a plan to make, it will be given to you. It may not be the plan your ego had hoped for, but it will always be the plan that your heart desires, one that serves your true needs and those of the world. If there are answers you need, you will receive them. Though they may not be the answers that your ego thought it needed, they are answers to another kind of question, a burning question that will become more and more alive in you until the answer is finally revealed.

The Power of Humility

"And the secret of letting to is...?"

Humility. Humility is the quality that puts you into a state of receptivity that makes letting go natural. When you identify with the false self, your mind goes into a frenzy and tries to manipulate the universe and tell Life how things should be. Humility takes you out of the false self into your True Self, into a state of unconditional love, and then you begin to flow with the universe.

Gratitude emerges spontaneously as you bask in the energy field of love. It releases a flow of spiritual energy that walks ahead of you and exerts a mighty influence in your life, setting up events and situations that are so advantageous they are beyond your wildest imaginings.

Develop a Grateful Mind

Remember, therefore, the Path of Gratitude. Focus on it constantly. Pray for gratitude, for it is the key to your salvation. You can be grateful that you are not wandering in the dark alone, for One Who Knows is constantly at hand, ready to guide you along the path that leads from death to eternal life. You can be grateful that your True Nature never changes and yet is full of purpose. You can be grateful that you are willing to transcend what you have made, your meager rewards and petty judgments, which is all your small mind has created so far in your life. Do not rest until you know yourself once more as the Source. Be vigilant and train yourself to replace anger and resentment with gratitude. Recognize that negative feelings do not serve your true good; they badger your ceaselessly and coerce you with no thought or care for you or for your future. Lift your heart above despair and become increasingly trusting in your True Self, knowing that you need no longer look anxiously backwards or forwards. Perfect love awaits you, here in the present moment.

Give thanks for every living thing, otherwise, you will have given thanks for nothing. Either you see the infinite value of every aspect of your world, or you do not truly see any value at all. Give thanks for your love and for your spiritual awareness. Give thanks for the greatest adventure ever, the journey within.

Cultivate a grateful attitude so that you can at last appreciate life. Develop a grateful mind, which is a peaceful mind, and draw to yourself great things. Give thanks for everything you are and everything you are experiencing. Let gratitude become the single thought that purifies the insane belief that you are separate from the Light. Let your soul sing a song of gratitude for your Wholeness and let it dance through life with Light steps, giving all its gifts with love.

Be grateful and be healed. A healed mind no longer bears the terrible burden of planning. Instead, it carries out effortlessly and with complete trust the plans that it receives by listening to your True Self within. A healed mind, when it is uncertain what to do, waits. When instruction comes, then it acts upon the information in full confidence. It gives up all compulsion for personal planning and follows only the assignments that are given to it. The healed mind is secure in the knowledge that all obstacles will be removed from its path. As it seeks to serve the master plan established for the highest good of every being, love prepares the way.

Practice

1) Do your daily meditation.
2) At the end of your meditation period, begin your Affirmation Session.

TEXT 1 — THE SETTING

Take a deep breath, relax, and align yourself with your breathing. Listen to your breath as it flows in and out of your body. Now visualize yourself entering a pyramid. This is your secret sanctuary, and it is filled with stillness and peace. You sit down on a beautiful throne that is the perfect design for you, and perfectly comfortable. The only energies in this pyramid are your own inner energies. You are completely protected from the external world.

TEXT 2 — THE INVOCATION

I invoke the energy of all the angels, archangels and masters. I call on the violet flame to consume, dissolve and purify all my dense thoughts and emotions. I ask for the release of any tendency to be attached, for my attachments are what inhibit the flower of love and separate me from the Light.

TEXT 3 — THE AFFIRMATIONS

- I am grateful for this day; whatever transpires I face with love and understanding.
- I perform every task with a grateful attitude, thankful that I can be used, that the channel is open and I can be of service.
- I am grateful that the Light in me awakens the Light in all.
- I am grateful my mind is absolutely committed to everything that is real
- I am grateful that I'm willing to create a future unlike the past.
- I am grateful that nothing external to me can hurt or injure me.

- I am grateful that everything is already decided for me by my True Self, and that I cannot undo what has been done.
- I am grateful for the priceless gift of spiritual awareness.
- I am grateful that the path I walk in life leads only to Love.
- I am grateful I know no law except the law of Love.
- I am grateful I am the Love that illumines the entire universe.

Harnessing the Sacred Power of Stillness

Peace is a natural attribute of your mind, but you have lost your awareness of it. To reclaim your natural state of inner peace, you have first to quiet the mind and listen. You will then discover that wherever you are and whatever circumstances you're in, however chaotic, your True Self accompanies you always. It is a soothing balm that heals you and heals the world. To access this place of utter tranquility, take a deep, soothing breath and allow your awareness to drop beneath your surface thoughts, like a diver sinking beneath the waves into the otherworldly stillness of an ocean.

This stillness is part of your True Nature, and so you are never completely disconnected from it. Have you ever been in a frantic situation and suddenly given up? All at once, you feel totally at peace, even though the situation has spun out of control. It happens when your worrying mind has exhausted itself and for a brief moment, your intrinsically peaceful presence has an opportunity to emerge.

Don't make the mistake of supposing that this stillness is something pleasant but ineffectual. It is, in fact, infinitely wise and strong. When you harness its sacred power, your life's problems simply melt away. You know exactly what to think, say, and do in any situation, and, though you cannot predict the exact outcome of any given set of events, you are unshakably certain that everything is unfolding in the perfect way.

A Tangible Example

One summer, my friend Jonathan's plane from Switzerland arrived late at London's Heathrow airport, leaving him with thirty minutes to go from Terminal One to Terminal Four in order to catch a transatlantic flight. From past experience, he knew this was possible, but when he turned a corner and came across a line of five hundred people waiting to board a bus with a fifty-passenger capacity, his optimism evaporated. Since he was scheduled to attend a ten-day event that was starting the next morning in California, he fell upon an airport worker and pleaded for special treatment. But to no avail.

His mind started racing, "What am I going to do?"; "Would British Airways have room for me on another plane?"; "Would they even take responsibility for the missed connection?" On and on his mind went. (You know what the mind's capable of when it goes into overdrive). Then he suddenly went blank. He had thought his way to a standstill, and all at once, he didn't know what else to think. A delicious sensation of absolute tranquility crept over him. It no longer mattered in the slightest whether he made the connection or not. The event in California would take place just fine without him, and the world would continue turning whether he spent the next few days in England or America.

Having no clue about what to do, he simply stood in the concourse and waited, at peace even though his hopes and plans were apparently in ruins. Then, out of the corner of his eye, he noticed some unusual activity: a group of young men and women in red uniforms was boarding a private bus. He had no clue who these people were or where they were going. He just knew he had to get on their bus. Ignoring the protests of the airport staff, he sprinted toward the vehicle and jumped onto it, just before the doors closed and it pulled away. He looked about and discovered that he had joined a troupe of charming ballet dancers from Mexico City, who enthusiastically applauded his antics. He learned that they were heading back to Mexico via Heathrow's Terminal Four, and therefore he was on the right bus and would make his connection.

The moral of the story is that when the mind is quiet, even for the unglamorous reason that it has thought itself to a standstill, events in the outside world can no longer make you anxious or afraid. Your tranquility is more powerful than anything that can happen to you. Although missing a connecting flight is insignificant compared with financial struggle, divorce, or loss, the principle still applies in every situation. What's more, a quiet mind lays out the red carpet for the miraculous: a situation that to a mind in turmoil appears unsolvable is very often suddenly resolved in an awe-inspiring way. The more proficient you become at harnessing the sacred power of stillness, the more you witness this phenomenon taking place in your life. When you are still, you're present, and this state of presence connects you with the unlimited wisdom, love, and strength of your True Self. To your rational mind, the result looks like a miracle, but from the perspective of your True Self, it's just business as usual.

The Miraculous is for Everyone

> *"All of this seems like it must apply to other people, not to me."*

It applies to everyone, including you. You can feel perfectly at ease, perfectly confident, perfectly joyful, and inexpressibly grateful in every moment, twenty-four hours a day. You can watch your life unfold as gracefully and effortlessly as a rose opening in the sun. You were born to experience this. It isn't something reserved for special people at special times. It's for all people at all times.

> *"Why don't I experience this, then? It's not as if I haven't been trying."*

You've been searching for peace without finding it because you believe that you can only have peace once your external circumstances arrange themselves in a way that is conducive to a peaceful existence. But this perfect arrangement of circumstances is never going to happen. To have peace, you must become aware of it now, regardless of what's happening outwardly, and in order to become aware of it you have to go within. You carry inside you what Paramahansa Yogananda, the founder of the Self Realization Fellowship, called a "portable paradise." Look for this inner Heaven and you will find it. When you live in your surface mind, you're living in a state of confusion born of fear. But when you dwell within the impenetrable walls of your portable paradise, you are in a state of abiding peace.

You don't see the paradise shining inside you there and it's intended for you. You just have to accept it and claim it. When you're aware of the paradise within, you naturally extend it to others, and then life becomes a celebration in which you gather with others in peace. To attain this idyllic state, you must quiet the mind.

Listening

Once your mind is silent, you have to do one more thing: Listen. True listening is sacred. It means to hear with your heart so that Light, love, healing, and compassion pour out of you. It's easy to yap constantly, both in thought and speech, but yapping has no value. Only thoughts and words emanating from the stillness are worthwhile.

Your True Self awaits your silence and is waiting for you to let go of chaos because you cannot hear your True voice while there are noise and confusion in your mind. Constant daily practice is needed to quiet the mind, so that your True Self's peace, love, and wisdom, which transcends your mental understanding, can come to you.

Don't Procrastinate

I'll start first thing in the morning."

Start today.

"Why?"

Because today is the day your True Self has created, and so that's where you can find yourself. Tomorrow is the day you made; you won't find your True Self there. Yesterday is the day you wasted, and you won't find yourself there either. So make today count.

Walk the Road to Peace

> *"When I was a kid, I witnessed my mother and father worrying about everything: money, illness, their relationship, the weather, you name it. I realized at an early age that worrying was an utterly pointless activity, and I swore that when I grew up I wouldn't be like my parents, that I'd live in a state of peace. I made that vow thirty years ago, and guess where I am today. My own children would certainly say that I'm much less peaceful than their grandparents."*

Yes, and they too are probably swearing that they won't turn out like you. Being from a more aware generation, maybe they will be able to keep their vow, but why wait to find out? Why don't you yourself snap the chain that keeps the generations tied together in misery?

The Truth is that you never have to worry about anything. Consider the lilies of the field, how they grow; they toil not, neither do they spin. These True words have resonated around the world for over two thousand years without any loss of impact. Whether you consider yourself a Christian or not is immaterial. You know in your heart of hearts that Life, given the opportunity, will support and protect you. Reflect on your life: Have any of the things you worried about actually turned out the way you feared they would? You may have experienced loss, deprivation, and heartache, but your life has shown remarkable resiliency, hasn't it? You've always bounced back, stronger than before.

So when you find yourself becoming anxious, depressed or agitated, remind yourself of the Truth in these terms: "He who sent me will direct me, but this can only happen if I stop the confusion in my mind. I could do what I always do, which is to substitute my own chaotic fears for the quiet wisdom, but I've been going down that road for years and it doesn't lead anywhere that I want to go. Today is the day that I'm going to try something different. I will sit in silence and discover that I am not alone, that One Who Knows accompanies me and, in silence, instructs me. As long as I continue to listen to my True Self in silence, I will know what to do and what to say. If I fall back into my old habits of anxious thinking, I will simply remember to listen in silence and once again hear my True Self's healing voice guiding me. If I become anxious ten thousand more times, I will remember to become quiet another ten thousand times. Whatever it takes, I will no longer be fooled by the thoughts of my small mind. If my family, my friends, and even my entire country continue to worship agitation and stress, I am still going to walk down the other road, the one that leads to eternal peace."

> *"I've been doing meditation for years, and it has definitely helped me become less stressed and more peaceful. But if I'm honest I'd say I'm still in an agitated state more of the time than not. The continual bliss you're alluding to seems Utopian."*

That's because the small mind goes through cycles of tension and release, causing you to experience periods of relative calm. Stillness, however, is quite different. It isn't evolved in intense or protracted form of what you already know; it is something entirely new that transforms you.

At present, your mind is still preoccupied with everything you experience. You keep judging your experiences, dividing them into good and bad, desirable and undesirable. You do this because you're protecting the identity you've made for yourself, in which you're someone who is alone and vulnerable. You imagine an outside world that is separate and hostile and then defend yourself from it. But, as the spiritual teacher Vernon Howard expressed it, "You're not who you think you are, and therefore you don't have the problems you think you have." This is why your only task is to discover who you are. This discovery changes everything. You no longer judge events, because you see that they are effects—not causes. You see that everything that happens is for your highest good.

It's difficult for you not to pass judgment on what you're seeing on the surface because the basic compulsion of the mind is to judge. But you have to train yourself to witness experiences without attaching any meaning to them. Your True Self does not know fear didn't create your fear, you did. In order to have peace, you have to let go of fear. Allow your True Self within you to give your experiences meaning. Then you will stop looking with fearful eyes and instead see life through the eyes of love.

Why wait for Heaven? Your True Self is with you now. It can so easily be discovered, why wait to find it in the future? Your True Self is shining within you, and from your heart, it extends around the world, caressing and blessing every living thing. Its blessings remain in force forever, since whatever comes from your True Self is eternal. Peace destroys all that is ephemeral and valueless while refreshing and renewing every heart that it touches. Peace radiating from you reminds the world of what it has forgotten, and the world then returns the favor and leads you into increasingly deeper realms of peace.

When you recognize peace in yourself, you automatically share it with others because the peace can no more be contained in you than the ocean can be contained in a thimble. Your peaceful thoughts, untainted by the dream of the outside world, become the messages from your True Self.

"And to achieve this, I do what exactly?"

Practice peace. Observe your wandering thoughts and gently bring them back so that they align with your real thoughts. Do not stray. Let the Light within your mind guide your thoughts back home. Restore your True Nature by forgiving without limits, by absolving the whole world from what you thought it did to you. It is you, yourself, who made the world that did these things; so choose a different world, one that is innocent, sinless, and blessed. To do this, you have to drop your personality, which is the self-created image that you mistakenly think is real.

You have thought your way into a snake pit, but your True Self will lead you out of the pit if you permit it to do so. Giving your permission means shifting into an attitude of total acceptance in which you let all things remain exactly as they are, without judging them. If you do this, your mind will be quiet and then you will see how to enter the real world.

The Power of Decision

It's important that you make a definite decision that you want the quietness of peace. Your present state of indecision sends life a confused message, with the result that life cannot help you. Your indecision is fueled by your fear of stepping out in faith and doing what needs to be done.

> *"What does that mean exactly, 'stepping out in faith and doing what needs to be done'?"*

For example, when I organize a weekend retreat, I usually get calls from several students saying, "I don't have the money," or "I have an important business meeting on Saturday," or "I've been working all week, I'm tired." These people are generally being tested. I don't mean that there's never a good reason to cancel your reservation for one of my events, but generally, the cancellation results from a person's lack of commitment to his or her spiritual growth. Since "spiritual growth" means greater peace, joy, and fulfillment, the only victim of this lack of commitment is the person who's being indecisive. There's nothing wrong with a conscious choice to save money, attend a business meeting, or stay in bed all weekend, but when you consistently make these options your priority, you're sabotaging yourself.

In this type of situation, I get tested too. Sometimes the rental cost for the venue is quite high, and then I'm tempted to waver and say, "I might not break even, so let's just forget about this weekend." However, I refuse to let whatever is appearing in the world of form influence me. If I see in consciousness that the weekend is to happen, then I don't interfere, and the retreat goes on. If I see that the decision has already been made in the invisible world, I don't second-guess it, because I've discovered that when I trust life, it always proves itself entirely trustworthy and leads me to increasingly glorious outcomes.

"Why are we always being tested?"

It's how you are strengthened. Each time you choose the Light, you grow. Conversely, each time you yield to the dictates of the small self, you become weaker. So you have to ask yourself, "Am I going to give in to the illusion—or am I going to stand up for the Truth?"

The illusion confuses and distracts you, but it is unreal. Bless the illusion, give thanks for it, and then move on without allowing it to interfere. As soon as you make a definite decision in your mind that you want your true life back, the universe will cooperate with you in marvelous ways.

The Voice of Your Heart

"How do I open the door to all these marvelous possibilities?"

The door has always been open for you, and it's still open now. You can, if you want, hang a curtain over the door and pretend it's not there. That's denial. If someone then comes along and informs you that the door to eternity lies behind your curtain, you can tell yourself he's lying or deceiving himself. Another strategy might be to agree that the door is where he says it is, but declare that you're too bad or ignorant to walk through it. Whatever tact you take, you're resisting the Truth, which results in fear. You no longer hear the voice of your True Self, and instead, substitute the voice of your small self, and the more you do this, the more fearful and resistant you become. The more you listen to the voice of fear, the more difficult it becomes to listen to the voice of your heart.

"How do I recognize the voice of my heart?"

When you hear the voice of your heart, you're being addressed directly, for it's speaking to the sacredness and the Wholeness that you are. The innocence within you is speaking to you. The more you sit quietly and listen, the more you understand that you are everything and everything is you. That's true transformation. It's the pathway that leads to eternal joy.

The Home Within

You cannot experience peace if you're holding onto the past. You can only experience peace in the present. Don't look back with regret or resentment, and don't look ahead in fear. Just look around you now, in awareness. Your grievances and anxieties hide your Light. So you have to let the past go completely, right down to the last detail. If you want to be at peace, drop the past and accept that you have no command over the future. Train your mind to remember your True Self. You are a child of love and not of fear. Fear in the mind produces fear in your life, whereas love in your mind produces love in your life. Choose love.

You can't know love unless you are living in peace. Have you ever seen a person being fearful and genuinely loving at the same time? It can't happen anymore than a pond can be troubled and still at the same time. Fear is an expression of your selfish nature, whereas love is an expression of your selfless nature. Love means putting the other person first; it means moving yourself out of the way so that the Truth of who you are can reveal itself to you; it means preventing your mind from being preoccupied with senseless, empty, valueless thoughts. If you're not living in peace, you're not extending love.

Start Anywhere

> *"So, to be loving I need to be peaceful and to be peaceful I need to be loving. Where am I supposed to start?"*

Actually, you can start anywhere.

> *"Isn't that giving us too much choice?"*

It seems confusing because you're thinking in terms of time, in which there are chains of cause and effect, one thing leading to another. The qualities that pertain to your True Nature — peace, love, wisdom, compassion, joy, and so on — are not in time, they are in eternity. They are not separate; they are indivisible parts of a whole. Therefore, when you walk through the doorway that leads to one of these qualities, you automatically access all of them. That's why you can begin anywhere.

Cultivating Peace of Mind

To live in peace, you cultivate a quiet mind. If your mind is agitated, it means you're seeing with physical eyes, and if you're seeing with physical eyes, you're not truly seeing. Eyes that look are common but eyes that see are rare, which is why there are so few noble people in history who have left their mark upon the Earth. These rare individuals made their mark because they let go of the past, relinquished command of future results, and lived in the present. In stillness, they became aware of the divine ideas arising within them and thus they played to the full their part in their True Self's plan.

A peaceful mind does not plan. Instead, it carries out the plan that it receives through listening the wisdom that is not its own. Currently, you're carrying out your own plan, not your True Self's plan. But your plan brings confusion, whereas True Self's plan brings peace. So, invite the True Self into your life. When you do this, nothing can destroy your peace of mind because your True Self goes with you wherever you go. Call out to your True Self and find the stillness, safety, and happiness you seek. When you call out to your True Self, you invite the angels to surround the ground on which you stand and sing to you as they spread their wings to keep you safe and shelter you from every worldly thought that would intrude upon your Wholeness and your True Nature.

> *"I have on occasions called out to the Light of my True Self, and I feel a peaceful presence within me. But it doesn't stay long, and then I'm left in my usual state of low-grade worry."*

The first thing to realize is that your True Self doesn't leave you; you leave your True Self. You're free to place your attention wherever you want, and you have chosen to place it in the chaotic negativity of the outer world. You don't see you're doing this, but you're doing it nevertheless. The constant activity going on within your mind deludes you into believing that you are separate from the Source of Life; as a result, even when you hear the "still small voice within" speaking to you, you dismiss what you hear and substitute your own self-made ideas.

Silence truly is golden; it's the language of the soul. To be still and do nothing is one of the highest virtues, for only a still mind is divine. The divine lies within you, but it is not something you can figure out, make happen or give as an experience to someone else. It is independent of time and thus beyond the intellect. The only thing you can do is enter into the stillness, and in that silence, you'll know the Truth directly.

Try it now. Be still an instant and go home. There's no need to experience a perpetual state of discontent. In your heart, you know this world is not where you belong; stop chasing rainbows, and find the home within. Your true home is the light within, which is a moment beyond time in which there are no movements or thoughts except those of your True Self. Your True Self's appeal to you is to recognize what has been given to you — beauty, joy, and peace.

Remove pettiness and selfishness from your mind, for silence is the absence of the small you. Drop your false beliefs and discover the knowledge that is already within you, the real knowledge that flows from the Light.

It has taken time for you to become what you're not. But it takes no time to be what you are. Can you end the constant activity that keeps you attached to form? Can you still your meaningless desires and become aware of the True Self that is your constant companion? Can you reach beyond words into the silence that has no name or form?

"Won't this stillness mean an end to life as I know it?"

It'll put an end to everything you don't truly want — your anxieties, insecurities, jealousies, doubts, and so on. But as far as your everyday, practical life is concerned, far from ending that life, the stillness will improve it beyond recognition. As Einstein pointed out, all great ideas originate in the silence of the mind, where you can hear your True Self's voice without any interference from your own thoughts and desires. That's where true intelligence can be found.

Many scientists and great thinkers have the humility to recognize that they are not the source of their own ideas. But there are also many great intellectuals who believe that this is nonsense and that the human brain, armed with reason and the almighty scientific method, is capable of ultimately unlocking all the secrets of the universe without needing to conjure up the divine intelligence of an imaginary self. It's not possible for a person who makes these arguments to understand a true response to them since to do so require the dissolution of the intellectual mind, which is the very last thing that the person would be prepared to do or even accept as a possibility. True spiritual teachings are making a very radical statement, far more radical than most individuals, including brilliant academics, can tolerate. The teachings assert that the person trying to understand reality isn't real. Only when the person questions the unquestionable — namely his cherished sense of identity — can he begin to make a genuine breakthrough into Truth.

> *"This identity that we're so attached to does seem impressively real."*

But it isn't. It's no more real than a character in a dream. You have to wake up to understand that this is so. Your True Self lives within you as a quiet presence awaiting your return from your self-created world to the real world that holds out to you in love. Be still and hear the healing voice. In silence, you nourish your soul, which cannot find rest in anything but love.

> *"I practice and practice and still, I do not spend much time in silence or at peace."*

Your mind is a problem-solving machine and as soon as it solves a problem, it generates a dozen more in order to remain constantly active. You are caught up in doing rather than being, in action rather than awareness. In meditation, listen very quietly, not agreeing nor disagreeing, but listening with complete attention. When your mind is still, you will listen out of time into the eternal now. In the world of time, you live a false life with other people; in timelessness, you live a true life with your True Self. A mind in time is in turmoil — always solving, planning, worrying, assessing, evaluating, analyzing, and investigating. This depletes your energy and detracts from the beauty of your face, the beauty of your movements, the beauty of your voice, and the beauty of your life.

Rule your mind, which you alone must rule, instead of allowing it to use you. Your mind is sticky like a spider's web; it needs to be unglued from the past and the future so that it can return to the stillness of the present moment. When you live in that stillness, which means to live in the Light, every moment is sparkling and precious, and every second is a miracle.

Practice

Suggestions for Quieting the Mind

Select a mantra from any sacred text and use it diligently with sustained effort. It is not vain repetition. Each repetition is transforming consciousness; it's ending the past and bringing you to the eternal present. It goes before you as you make the journey back to the Light. You do not need to follow anyone's method or technique, nor do you need to sit in meditation for long hours and accomplish nothing. Give your True Self an instant and join with yourself completely. Each of us will progress at his or her own pace. There is no failure except the failure to practice faithfully. There is no formula; just be willing to practice. There are many obstacles on your path. They are there to strengthen you. Be patient with yourself. Darkness and turmoil is not your natural state. Read spiritual texts reverently and slowly so that you can harness the Light energy in the words, driving it deep into your consciousness to dissolve all that does not belong there.

Once you have discovered your True Self in the depths of meditation, then you see the divine Source of Life everywhere, in everything, and in everyone, expressing itself in millions and billions and trillions of different forms.

1) Do your daily meditation.
2) At the end of your meditation period, begin your affirmation session.

TEXT 1 — THE SETTING

Take a deep breath, relax, and align yourself with your breathing. Listen to your breath as it flows in and out of your body. Now visualize yourself entering a pyramid. This is your secret sanctuary, and it is filled with stillness and peace. You sit down on a beautiful throne that is the perfect design for you, and perfectly comfortable. The only energies in this pyramid are your own inner energies. You are completely protected from the external world.

TEXT 2 — THE INVOCATION

I invoke the energy of all the angels, archangels and masters. I call on the violet flame to consume, dissolve and purify all my dense thoughts and emotions. I ask for the release of any tendency to be attached, for my attachments are what inhibit the flower of love and separate me from my True Self.

TEXT 3 — THE AFFIRMATIONS

- I am calm, quiet, confident, and assured.
- I am released from conflict.
- I am drinking from the waters of peace.
- All that is weak is being burnt away.
- I see all things in terms of love.
- I ask for complete and total protection to see my True Self, my "I AM" presence.
- All of my thoughts are purified.
- I recognize the universal force behind the world, the invisible power that flows through matter.
- All that is not of Light is melting away, like mist in the sun.
- Nothing happens without my consent.
- I am responsible for my thoughts.
- I am liberating myself from slavery.
- My life is no longer regulated by anything external.
- I love myself unconditionally.
- I am listening in the silence.
- I am listening with my heart.

Choose one of the above affirmations and repeat it as often as possible during the day. Set the intention of making the spiritual Truth contained in the affirmation change your life.

Love

All you really want is to love and be loved. You are hungry for love, and you can have it if you look for it in the right place. The New Testament says, "Seek ye first the Kingdom of Heaven and all else shall be added unto you" (Matthew 6:33 KJV), for as long as you look outside yourself for love, you will not find it. But when you unglue the mind you discover love, which is your True Nature, concealed within, then you can look outwards and find love everywhere.

Letting Love In

At present, you are making an error that is causing you to be disconnected from your Source. Your task is to acknowledge this error and correct it. The correction you make is for your True Self, not for other people. You're doing it solely for your own benefit. Don't be concerned whether your neighbor is correcting his error; just focus on your own path home. Now is the time for you to dance in the Light, to become what you are — infinite love. Now is the time to come home.

All you are asked to do is to let love in, for it waits on welcome, not on time. Stop blocking love and simply recognize its presence here and now. Give of your love freely, for it is endlessly abundant. The more you appreciate your life, the more you love; the more you love, the more you have to give; and the more you give, the more you receive. Every experience is teaching you more about loving, giving and receiving.

> *"If love is what I want above all things, why on earth would I block it?"*

You block love because you're unconsciously afraid that it will deprive you of what you think you want. You have mental images of what love is — all of them inaccurate — and then you react to these images with fear, as if they were real. If you only knew how inestimably desirable the presence of Love is in our life, you wouldn't care what apparent sacrifices it required. What's more, you'd soon discover that the only things you're being asked to surrender are the illusions that are causing you to suffer.

Let go of your fears, and love will immediately appear. There are no good fears, because they all block love, and so you should drop them all indiscriminately. Your small mind will resist, telling you that you need the fears, but you know what answer to give.

> *"I want something absolutely different in my life now, and I'm giving up everything that has clearly not served me, including fear."*

Of course, I'm not referring to biological fear, which releases adrenaline and prepares the body to avoid danger. This is a natural part of your physical experience. The problem is the psychological fear that comes from your mistaken belief that you are the body and that if the body gets hurt or dies, you get hurt or die. This kind of fear perpetuates the illusion that you're a separate being, whereas true Love dispels this false perception and reveals the Wholeness that unites all things. You don't get to choose what's false and what's real, but you do get to choose which direction to take. You're faced with a simple fork in the road: one side leads to fear and suffering, the other leads to love and bliss. Those are your alternatives in every instant: love or fear.

Every problem in life results from the lack of love. What is darkness? Lack of love. What is sin? Lack of love. What is fear? Lack of love. Lack of love means that you have chosen wrongly. So choose again. Correct your error by letting love into your life. In every situation ask, "What would Love do now?" Trust in the process and you will receive loving guidance. By consistently following the Voice of Love, you will gradually build a bridge to your True Self.

Jumping into the Void

> *"I know what you're saying is good news, but it makes me feel despondent. I've been on a spiritual path for several decades, and I can't honestly say I've built a bridge to my True Self, even though in public I pretend that I have."*

The more "spiritual" we are, the more difficult it is to drop our self-images and allow reality to take over. Is it easier for a billionaire to drop his self-importance than is it for a monk to do so, and thus replacing material importance with spiritual importance?

You're seeing your pretense, at least, and that's a good place to start. It's also a frightening place to start because beyond your spiritual belief system, you see nothing but emptiness. You have to find the courage to jump into the void, and this requires leaving behind everything you've ever believed, spiritual or otherwise.

> *"And to summon up this* courage, *I do what?"*

Take a good look at what's growling at you: that's a lion, not a kitty, at your heels, and it's going to devour you. When you see this unmistakably, jumping into the void doesn't seem so scary.

> *"Meaning?"*

Your fear and suffering are eating up your life. When you see this as clearly as you can see a dangerous animal snapping at you, you'll willingly jump into the unknown.

Turning on the Light

"And seeing clearly involves...?"

Asking yourself honestly, "Is my heart absolutely untouched by fear?"; Do I give to others without any sense of loss, but with profound joy?"; "Do I understand that giving is all and getting is meaningless?"; "Do I give continuously of my love, knowing that my love is endlessly abundant?" If you cannot unreservedly answer "yes" to these questions, then ask for help. Ask to be given the sincerity that will make you want the Truth more than you want the beliefs that keep you stuck in the illusion. Imagine you're in a dark room bumping into furniture and jumping with fright at every sound. A friend suggests that you turn on the Light. Are you going to continue giving your usual responses, "I'll get around to that later; right now I'm busy fending off all these things that keep attacking me"; or, "I've looked for the switch, and I can assure you there isn't any Light in this room" ; or, worst of all, "What are you talking about? The Light's already on."

"What would be a productive response, then?"

You could cry out with a sense of urgency, "Help me turn on the Light, and help me right now!"

"And what would I see once the Light was on?"

You'd see that you already are everything you want to be. You'd see that you are not your own creation, but are instead something infinitely precious that was created by your True Self. You'd understand that the real and the unreal are your only options, and you'd eagerly choose what is real.

At present the real is beyond your understanding, and therefore love is also beyond your understanding. However, you're not being asked to understand it; all you're being asked to do is to let it in, for love only enters when it is welcomed. You just need to stop rejecting it by placing a demand on it, and your True Self—which is Love—will become present in your life.

You see, it's the demands that you place on love that bring you sorrow, not love itself. Love cannot satisfy ego-conceived desires because, otherwise, it would be giving you what you don't truly want. Stop looking back to the past with resentment or ahead to the future with fear. Look around this present moment with awareness. Bring not one thing with you that the past has taught you. You've been badly taught! The past is over, a mere memory trace in your mind; don't let it trap you. Your True Self cannot give you fear or resentment because your True Self cannot give what it does not have and it cannot have what it is not. Your True Self is not fear, resentment, or any other kind of suffering. Your True Self exists in the present moment.

Your True Self is not to be found by any of your current methods of seeking, which are all locked in time. Love stands outside the body and the world, and it will appear to you when you voluntarily hand over your past to your True Self and allow yourself to receive your gifts. When you equate yourself with a body, you invite separation and pain to take up residence with you as long-term guests, and then love disappears.

The Action of Grace

"How do I transform my fear and pain into love?"

You can't! Fear can only live in fear, and whatever it directs the body to do is painful. Love can only live in love, and whatever it directs the body to do is joyful. The opposite of love is not fear, but love. Love begets love, whereas fear only begets fear. Therefore, you cannot transform one into the other.

When I say that the price of love is to give up your illusions, I'm using the word "price" ironically. Love cannot be purchased, stolen, ransomed, or seduced. It is not a business contract. It has no distinctions, degrees, levels, divergences, or separate parts. It does not alter with a person or circumstance; it is unchangeable. Its meaning lies in oneness. It is the heart of your True Self.

Step back and do not dwell upon the forms that keep you bound. You have mistaken your made-up creations for real Creation to such an extent that it is impossible for you to know anything truly. You deny yourself your divine inheritance, and so you dwell in a state of fear and lack.

Allow Grace to rescue you. Grace is your natural state. It is divine love and protection given to you by your True Self. When you are not in a state of grace, you're not living in the environment for which you were created, and everything then becomes a strain. You are only at ease when you know you are one with your True Self. Grace is a virtue coming from your True Self, who watches over you and denies you nothing, though you deny your True Self constantly. When you deny your True Self, you deny yourself. The remedy is to stop denying your True Self. As soon as you do this, Grace appears and fear vanishes.

Releasing Fear

Fear is simply a wrong idea. You think you can be hurt or destroyed, and that thought makes you afraid. But the thought is not real; it's part of the dream. Fear is evil wreaking havoc in your mind. Evil is the veil of darkness that clouds the mind and sends you to sleep.

All suffering is the absence of love. Therefore, where there is hatred, suspicion, despair, envy and fear — choose to plant love.

Fear makes appreciation of life impossible. If you are afraid of anything, you are acknowledging its power to hurt you, and thus you believe you are powerless. Every one of your unkind or harmful actions has been done when you felt powerless. Realize, then, that all power is of your True Self and what is not of your True Self has no power to hurt you. Stop giving power to that which is essentially powerless. Love is the only power. Love does not attack darkness; it simply brings Light to it. Whatever is exposed to Light becomes Light.

Surrender to the Light by unmasking the old program of fear and allowing the energies of your True Self to carry you. Strip away constantly all that is unreal. Every second is an opportunity to be the love that you are. So don't delay. Allow yourself to be woken up from the dream so that you can live in the real world, which is the world of love.

Returning Home

> *"Aren't we human beings just so burdened down with sin that it's impossible to live in a state of love?"*

Sin is an archery term meaning *to miss the mark*. Therefore, sin is an error — it's when you err from the Truth. The Prodigal Son erred away from his home and finally returned. Did his father tell him he'd been bad and condemn him to wander in the wilderness for another few decades? No, he welcomed him home with open arms. To be home is to be sinless. They're one, and the same thing. You're either erring or you're at home. You choose. You haven't been exiled as a punishment. When you decide to go home, you go home; it's as simple as that.

Sin obscures the soul. Get rid of the insanity that the world is ugly. The body's eyes were made to look on error, but the Love will correct all errors if you allow it. Everything that happens is what you desire, and everything that does not happen is what you do not want to occur. When you choose love instead of fear, you suddenly shift from the visible to the invisible, meaning you transcend body identification and achieve Spirit identification. This gives the impression that a miracle has taken place because anything that comes from Love is a miracle. Love ends suffering, and there is no greater miracle than that.

If you are overlooking love, you are overlooking yourself, because love is what you are. To recognize love, therefore, recognize that you are love. See the false as the false; suffering is not your True Nature;

it is only something that obscures it. Disappear into the presence beyond the veil, not to be lost but to return home to your True Self.

Choosing Joy

Do not let the false self's thoughts direct your words or actions. Be peacefully alert. When the false self's thoughts arise, quietly step back, examine them, and let them go. You do not want what they offer because they offer nothing. Choose the joy of your True Self's thoughts instead. This is your time to expand your consciousness and enter into a state of bliss.

"How do I choose joy?"

Choose to drop your grievances. You hold onto the past and nurse it as if it were some great treasure. To hold a grievance is to let the false self rule your mind, which means hiding the Light and denying that you were created by Love. Let the veil be lifted.

Take responsibility for your life. If you are not expressing love, joy, health, harmony, and abundance in your life, then you are disobeying divine principles. You choose the feelings your experience, you decide upon the goals you want to achieve, and you attract everything that happens to you. Since you receive everything you ask for, ask for what will strengthen you, not what will weaken you. Ask for love, because only love gives you strength.

All the so-called bad things that happen to you occur because of lack of love. Earn a Ph.D. in love and know infinite joy and fulfillment. The only lack is your illusion that the branch is separated from the vine. Do not support your neighbor's illusion in this regard, or you will once more perceive yourself as lacking. You see what you think you are, and what you think you are is what you become.

Seeing with Eyes of Love

See your neighbor as you see yourself, through eyes of love. When he treats you harshly, call on the love you both are so that you may both heal and strengthen. Allow no negative thoughts to enter your mind, regardless of the form of the experience. This is what Jesus meant when he said, "Turn the other cheek" and "Resist not evil." When he appealed to God, "Forgive them Father, for they know not what they do" (Luke 23:34 KJV), he was asking for their minds to be healed. You grow in love and wisdom by choosing to have compassion for others. Love and wisdom give you inner strength and balance, which you bring into the physical world so that you can handle any situation with patience and confidence.

True confidence, the kind that includes humility, is a sign of spiritual progress. If you are clinging to or resisting life, unwilling to simply accept things as they are, you are thrown into uncertainty. When you are confident, it means you have let go of your attachments to the past and are allowing the current of life to take you effortlessly toward a different future.

"Doesn't that make us become puppets without any self-direction?"

Not at all...for the first time, you will be truly self-governing. Life is a tremendous responsibility and your part in it is essential. You are a beacon of Love, bringing Light to the world.

"How do I become that?"

Remove your gaze from the form that keeps you bound and look inward with eyes of love. Allow your mind to return to its natural state. Let your intent be to die to the false so that the new can emerge. You sabotage yourself with your fearful thoughts because you do not think you are worthy of the joy that is rightfully yours. You are_worthy of it. It's your birthright. So claim it by letting go of everything that's not you. As Meister Eckhart, a great medieval mystic, put it, "In order to be what you want to be, you have to cease being what you are." We are here to transcend human consciousness and become enlightened. Enlightenment is not strictly speaking of a transformation, but rather the recognition of what you are, namely the living Light.

Beyond Practice

> *"And I can achieve this transcendence if I work diligently with the practice sections in this book?*

Don't be fooled by the apparent structure of *Ungluing the Mind.* It does have a structure, the real work is happening beneath the level of your awareness. Make sincere, conscious efforts, but realize that your mind as it is now cannot understand anything. It's your present state of mind that wants the comfort of a recognizable structure so that it can integrate the new into the old, and thus feel secure. You have to let go of everything, including all recognizable structures.

Don't try to live your life according to a plan or a schedule, it was not meant to be lived that way. Your life has one purpose, to remember your True Self and then express it in daily living. In the quiet of your mind, ask the question, "Who am I?" and wait patiently for the answer. In the stillness, the answer will reveal itself to you: You are love. When you hear this answer, you will recognize and understand it, not because you read it in a book or because someone told you, but because love can recognize itself.

As you go through the process of discovering who you are, you resemble a toddler learning to walk. You fall down, pick yourself up, and then fall down again. Don't ask, "Why did I make that mistake?" Ask only, "What have I learned from it?" Mistakes are a natural and inevitable part of your growth; they only lead to suffering when you resist learning from them. There's no satellite navigation to take you infallibly to your destination. Errors are inevitable; so welcome them.

Simply persist, and you will eventually enter into a state of Love. Then you'll no longer react to conditions or situations outside of yourself, but instead, you'll act from a place of unity. Every experience is an opportunity to dive more deeply into your True Nature so that you act from the consciousness of love instead of reacting from the consciousness of fear.

Acting from the consciousness of love, you are capable of transforming the planet. So why not decide in favor of both yourself and the world? Why not choose love?

Practice

1) Do your daily meditation.
2) At the end of your meditation period, begin your affirmation session.

TEXT 1 — THE SETTING

Take a deep breath, relax, and align yourself with your breathing. Listen to your breath as it flows in and out of your body. Now visualize yourself entering a pyramid. This is your secret sanctuary, and it is filled with stillness and peace. You sit down on a beautiful throne that is the perfect design for you, and perfectly comfortable. The only energies in this pyramid are your own inner energies. You are completely protected from the external world.

TEXT 2 — THE INVOCATION

I invoke the energy of all the angels, archangels and masters. I call on the violet flame to consume, dissolve and purify all my dense thoughts and emotions. I ask for the release of any tendency to be attached, for my attachments are what inhibit the flow of love and block me from my True Nature.

TEXT 3 — THE AFFIRMATIONS

- I am encircled by the protective presence of love.
- I am an unstoppable force of love.
- I am taking a bath in a pool of love.
- I am pouring upon my body temple the oil of love.

- I am radiating love in all directions endlessly.
- I am giving myself the gift of love.
- I am on a path of love, joy, and peace.
- I am showered with love and blessings.
- I am breathing in love and breathing out love.
- I am giving and receiving love freely, for I am love.

Choose one of the above affirmations and repeat it as often as possible during the day. Set the intention of making the spiritual Truth contained in the affirmation change your experience of life.

Enlightened Relationships

You do not have a genuine relationship with others for as long as you persist in the illusion that you are separate from them. What you think of as a relationship is usually a form of co-dependence, meaning that you use each other to create a sense of Wholeness. You mistakenly believe that the other person has something you need that you can only get from him or her. Though you may be unaware of the process, this sets up a situation in which, subtly or otherwise, you control and manipulate the other. This is because the emptiness you feel inside is so painful that you must fill it at all costs, and so you become afraid that the other person will stop cooperating with you. You want the other person to behave in certain ways that help you feel better. When they do this, you love them, but if they fail to correspond to your image of what you need from them, then watch out! Your love will quickly turn to hate. But love is clearly not love if it changes into hate. Love is changeless.

Relating to Yourself

For as long as you're invested in the world of form, you cannot love unconditionally. When you're attached to what is impermanent, then you are in a state of fear, and where there is fear, love is not. Therefore the question is: Can you relate to what does not change? Are you willing to accept your Divine power? Are you willing to bring about a radical transformation of your perception? Are you willing to wake up and know yourself as an aspect of the Light? Are you willing to co-create and be in joy? Or do you want to continue mis-creating and thus continue to suffer?

If you want a different life, then heal the distortion in your mind that views life as something outside of you. Be resolute in breaking free of the external world that has you mesmerized, trapped. To break free, you need to simply *be*. To be is to exist within the heart of your True Self. Being is love. Do you really want to live your life from this place of unconditional love? If so, are you willing to end all superficial activity and be in a whole relationship with yourself? Once you've accomplished this, then you can be in a real relationship.

Breaking the Vicious Cycle

> *"It sounds so simple, and yet all my relationships are so complex."*

That's because you're locked into a vicious cycle. Being afraid, you take action that's motivated by fear, which generates more fearful experiences, which makes you more afraid, which triggers more actions motivated by fear, and so on. You don't realize you're doing this. You think you're taking intelligent measures to deal with situations as they arise. You don't see that most of what you think, say and do is motivated by an extremely pervasive and insidious state of fear. Unconsciously, your fear drives you to make secret bargains in your relationships—I'll do this thing for you that makes you feel safe and good if you do this other thing for me that makes me feel safe and good. You even try to bargain with your True Self, but your True Self does not make bargains; your True Self knows only to give totally and does not need your advice or your suggestions.

Diving Beneath the Surface

> *"The usual question, then: What am I to do?"*

And here's the usual answer: Do the opposite of what you've been doing! But first, see what it is that you've been doing. You can't be in denial about this, or you'll get nowhere. See your fear. See that it propels you to grab some experiences and push others away. See that your whole life is about what's happening on the outside and that you know nearly nothing about the inside. See that you make yourself a victim of people and circumstances by giving them the power to determine how you feel. Be honest about the fact that you've reached this point in *Ungluing the mind* and still you have not decided to make the journey in the opposite direction, whatever the cost. When you do all this (not so much a doing, in fact, as a seeing), then you'll be on your way.

The wise always start with themselves. They look within. Dive beneath the surface and discover what's inside you. On the surface, where your self-created mind dwells, there is only a world of confusion, conflict, and illusions. Can you stop being deceived by the external world of form and instead accept what is not of this world- your True Nature? Until you do this, there will be no real, lasting joy in your life or your relationships.

"*Why do I have so many failed relationships?*"

Relationships break down not because you are bad but because you are illiterate in love. You do not know the meaning of love and that is your handicap. Identification with the physical is not a solid foundation on which to build a relationship. Love and control cannot exist in the same space. Everything is related to everything else. The unenlightened relationship, in which you identify a special other as the source of your wellbeing, is no relationship. It's based on differences, isolation, and separation. Unenlightened relationships produce confusion, and a confused mind cannot know the Truth. There is one life, one Source, one Truth, one love. Relate only to the oneness that will never leave you, has no missing parts, and knows nothing of differences. You and the other are both manifestations of the Light; therefore, you are the same, and in this sameness, you discover the Truth. A divided mind that believes it is separate from the Light cannot know love, because it cannot do anything but judge. Love is whole and free of judgment; it does not alter when a person or a thing changes. Loving is not something you do, it's something you simply allow to work through you. A divided mind is split, seeing everything in fragmented pieces floating on the surface of life. Dive for the pearls at the bottom of the sea. Then you will have a love to give that is not born of time but of eternity.

The Oneness of Life

Whether you are conscious of it or not, we are all connected in Truth. We are all one being, cleverly disguised to look separate. You hide in false relationships in order to perpetuate this illusion of separation. You want your relationship to serve your mistaken perception of who you are and what you want. But if you don't know who you truly are, then you don't know what you truly want. What you really desire is union with your True Nature. Once you achieve this all your relationships become filled with Light, because you are the Light. Therefore, love others not in terms of form or behavior but in terms of your inner Wholeness: your inner Light.

Sharing Love

When you are connected to the Light, you do not seek safety or power in the things of this world, for only your True Self has power, since only the real has a real effect. Dreams appear to have power, but when you awaken, has anything in the waking world changed? No, for the power of a dream evaporates the instant you become conscious. In a state of enLightenment, you know this and seek support only in what is real, only in the Light. Seeing your true power and glory in all things at all times, you constantly remember who you are, which is an eternal fountain of love. Imagine how your relationships would be if your sole objective were to share love. You get into conflict with others because you believe in separation; but when you see the Light in everyone, you see the Oneness, and your relationship with others is immediately transformed. You see no one person as special because you see everyone as unique because everyone is unique. You no longer identify another person as your only source of love and your sole opportunity for liberation, because you realize that everyone in every instant is a reflection of your True Self and an expression of freedom. You no longer divide the world into enlightened and unenlightened parts and instead experience every instant, person, place, thing, and action as inexpressibly whole. As a result, every moment of your life becomes precious and every encounter becomes a meeting with your True Self.

Ending Loss

When you operate from the Universal Mind instead of the false mind, losing love is impossible, just as it is impossible for the ocean to stop being wet. Because you know that you are love, you no longer need to snatch love from others. You do not have to manipulate another in order to get love nor do you have to be afraid that you will lose their love. When you see yourself as whole, you make no demands on others.

Perfect love exists eternally within you, and your recognition of this Truth is the antidote to the beliefs of your self-created mind that trick you into thinking you can gain and lose things and people. In the real world, there is no loss, only love; thus, you no longer feel compelled to get anything from any relationship or to use other people to complete yourself. The surprising consequence of this is that your relationships start to give you everything you desire, for relationships rooted in Wholeness are never in conflict and always satisfy you completely. Intimacy becomes more joyful than you ever dreamed possible.

De-cluttering Your Mind

"When I hear of these possibilities, I just feel so stuck."

It's your mind that's stuck. So let it come unglued! The glued mind, sticky with beliefs, takes control of you and keeps you imprisoned. Conversely, a free Mind, one that's not stuck together with mistaken perceptions, is under the command of your True Nature. When you're free, you use the mind rather than allowing it to use you. The mind returns to its proper function only when it is willing to know. Empty your mind so you can relate to what does not change, and thus enter into a true relationship with yourself. Situations, events, and circumstances change, but what you are does not change; it's eternal. When you understand this, you'll see that everyone else is the same as you.

Looking into the Mirror of Relationship

So, whoever you may be blaming or condemning now, remind yourself, even if you don't entirely believe what you're saying, that they're not harming you. In fact, they're your teachers, because they're showing you to yourself. They don't have to be aware of their role as your teacher to be effective. They simply have to be part of the universe because the entire universe is your teacher, acting as a mirror. Look into the mirror and see what you're actually doing. Be prepared for a shock. Go ahead and look anyway.

The Nature of Lasting Love

> *"When you are coming from an unconditionally loving place, does this mean that our intimate relationships will endure? Will there be an end to the heartbreak of separation and divorce?"*

Yes and no. We want our relationships to last forever, and they do at the level of being. On this level, they are continuous, but in the world of form they are always changing. You can't avoid this because, as the Greek philosopher Heraclitus so succinctly put it, "the only constant is change." Therefore, stop looking for permanency in a world whose only permanent feature is that it changes. Don't give up and resign yourself to a life of misery. Start looking for what is truly permanent - your inner Light- which is so close to you that you've forgotten it's there.

What we're all searching for is the Light, which brings with it infinite joy, wisdom, and fulfillment. Perhaps you feel you have strayed so far from the Light that, before returning to it, you need infinite forgiveness. But you don't have to be forgiven and you don't have to forgive yourself. All you have to do is awaken from the dream, and for this you need to love yourself because love can only be awakened by love.

Accept Humility

"And the secret for awakening?"

Be willing to wake up. In your current state, you can't awaken by yourself, but you can have an open mind that wants to learn the Truth. Having an open mind is so simple that you can have one instantly, right now, if you choose. Say to yourself, "For a little while, I'll entertain the possibility that I don't know or understand anything. If a knowing, understanding or judging thought enters my mind, so be it. I'll nevertheless remain aware of the fact that I actually might not know anything." At present, you can't learn because you secretly think you already know everything. Look back over your past: How many times have you reacted in the same way to the same situation and obtained the same unpleasant results? For example, how many times have you perceived someone to be "wrong", argued with them so that they can appreciate what's "right", and failed to achieve anything other than having an argument and the bad feelings that accompany it? In other words, how many times have you tried to get to the other side of the locked door by banging your head against it, and ended up each time with nothing but a headache? Have the honesty to see that you do this. It's going to be humiliating because you're going to see that you've been acting in an insane manner, that is, repeating the same action over and over and each time expecting different results. Allow yourself to feel humiliated; it's a sign that you're beginning to see things as they are.

The Truth is that everything you've always thought to be true has never been true. Yes, this is a radical, even shocking, statement. But if what you thought you knew was capable of bringing you permanent joy, a deep sense of purpose, and effortless fulfillment, don't you think it would have achieved this by now? Let go of all your beliefs; so far, in your life, they haven't taken you where you want to go. What gain is there in clinging to them? If you focus on beliefs that cannot give you true understanding, you emphasize your helplessness. But you're not helpless; you're a child of love and you have the boundless power of Wholeness on your side. You are emerging from an illusion of what you think you are into the acceptance of your True Self. Until you awaken to the joy of your True Nature, you'll keep on searching, but you'll be searching in the wrong place.

Seeking Wisely

One moonless night, a man was on his hands and knees looking for something in the grass at the base of a lamppost. A woman walked by and asked if she could help. "Yes," the man replied, "I've lost my keys." The woman knelt beside him and helped with the search. After a few minutes, she said, "Are you sure you dropped them here?" Pointing back down the street, the man answered, "Oh no, I dropped them over there, but under this lamppost is the only place where I can see anything." Stop looking in the wrong place just because, for now, it's all you can see. Your True Self is not found outside you. When you look through the body's eyes, there is little joy in your life or your relationships because your physical eyes see only error. Seek wisely with spiritual eyes and you will see the love that you are. This love will heal you.

Using Relationships for Self-Awareness

"What is the purpose of a relationship?"

Every relationship is an opportunity for growth, an opportunity to remember who you are. If you are remembering the identity you have created for yourself, you are remembering nothing. Your self-made image has never gotten you anywhere. It has never accomplished anything that proved to be a true success, and it never will. Your small identity exists only in your dream, and nothing you do in the dream fundamentally changes anything for you. Only awakening from the dream matters. For your self-created mind this is a frightening idea but embrace it anyway. It's one of the keys to your liberation. This is why the theme of this book is to unglue the mind. When you unglue the mind, you immediately become aware of your True Nature, which is to be connected with the Light. When you unglue the mind, your journey back to the Light is over.

"What makes a relationship enlightened?"

In an enlightened relationship, you are not looking to the other person, and the other person is not looking to you. You are both looking within and are dependent only on the Source that gave your life. In an enlightened relationship, one person does not dominate another. When you feel pain and anguish in relationships, that is selfishness aching to have its own way. When you do not have your way, your self will is violated and you flare up. But when you can extinguish self will, and become aware of who you are, your anger turns into joy and wisdom. Every relationship has the potential to bring you to the awareness of who you are, and so every relationship properly perceived is an enlightened relationship. In fact, there is only ever one relationship: the one with yourself, with your True Self. All external relationships are designed to help you return to your original state. Realizing this, you recognize that you live in a blessed world in which relationships without limits have been given to you; every time you meet someone, you see in them the Truth of who they are. In this way, every encounter, however apparently trivial, becomes an enlightened encounter that frees you from illusion, because, by seeing the Light in others, you are liberated from time. By offering Light to others, you become enlightened. By offering love, you become love.

Your True Nature is Love

> *"I try to be truly loving, but it's so hard to maintain a state of unconditional love."*

Start by becoming more intimate with yourself. You exist in relationship with others so that you can get back in touch with your True Nature. When you do this, you automatically withdraw your selfish desires from the relationship, which leaves you free to love, give support and strengthen the other person, without effort. You are able to build an enlightened relationship that is rooted in the eternal, and so endures forever.

Decide what you truly want. Nothing can oppose your single-minded determination. Do you want your relationships to be host to your True Nature or hostage to your ego nature? Since, to your True Nature, giving is all, while getting is meaningless, in every relationship ask only, "What can I give?" When an attitude of unconditional sharing underlies a relationship, then you have constructed a palace in which unconditional love will take up residence. You are either functioning from love or fear. If your mind perceives without love, it is unaware of the True Self within. When you know you are love, then that is what you share. And what you share comes back to you: give out fear, and it will come back to you; give out love, and it will be returned to you increased a thousand fold.

Your true being, your True Nature, is love. Your True Nature is complete. It takes you beyond your physical senses and your rational mind to the timeless present, to a consciousness where the language of love is unspoken and yet understood. Therefore, just be. As you allow yourself to be, your relationships will automatically heal.

Difficulty = Disconnection

> *"I wish I could believe that "being" will heal my relationships, but my family is in chaos. My husband and children argue constantly, and I usually end up in the middle. In the everyday world I live in, I don't see how my just 'being' is going to lead to healing; at least not without a big shift on the part of the other members of the family".*

Focus on seeing the Truth yourself. You do not need cooperation from others they are already cooperating with you perfectly. If you stop judging them and consider what they're showing you, you'll discover that they're revealing to you your own disconnection from the Light. When you are connected to your Source, nothing and nobody troubles you. So when you find yourself being troubled, be grateful. You're being shown that you still believe in separation. Stop focusing outwards on others and start looking within. Use your inner vision to recognize that every being is part of the whole and the whole is in every being. It's perfectly natural to see this, for it is the way your True Self thinks, and what is natural to your True Self is all natural to you. Learn to see this way, and you will discover that the spark of Light is safe, however hidden it may be, in every relationship.

Every Relationship is Perfect

When you are challenged, remember to persist, be determined, and pray. Prayer is a state of mind in which you experience Wholeness. Look out from the perception of your own Light to the Light of others. There are only two choices—darkness or Light— and your choice determines what you see. Remember that every encounter, whether with family, friends, acquaintances, or strangers, is an enlightened encounter. As you see the other, you will see yourself; as you think of him, you will think of yourself; for in him you will find yourself or lose yourself.

Because your mind is split, you see everything in the world of form as either enlightened or unenlightened. You judge things and people as being positive or negative according to your small self's mistaken idea about what it wants and doesn't want. In reality, all relationships are exactly perfect, all relationships are enlightened. See your family and every other person who enters your life, through the eyes of the Light. Remember that the Light is found not in time but in timelessness, and so turn your gaze away from time and separation and accept the eternal Wholeness of your True Self's love.

Place your trust in the Light, for it is the only investment that never fails. Creation already is enlightened. All that is missing is for you to remember that you are the Divine Creation and that your nature is the Light itself. Do this and watch all your relationships blossom. Remember who you are. Behind all your doubts, past all your fears, the one true relationship is yours for the asking.

Practice

1) Do your daily meditation.
2) At the end of your meditation period, begin your affirmation session.

TEXT 1 -THE SETTING

Take a deep breath, relax, and align yourself with your breathing. Listen to your breath as it flows in and out of your body. Now visualize yourself entering a pyramid. This is your secret sanctuary, and it is filled with stillness and peace. You sit down on a beautiful throne that is the perfect design for you, and perfectly comfortable. The only energies in this pyramid are your own inner energies. You are completely protected from the external world.

TEXT 2- THE INVOCATION

I invoke the energy of all the angels, archangels and masters. I call on the violet flame to consume, dissolve and purify all my dense thoughts and emotions. I ask for the release of any tendency to be attached, for my attachments are what inhibit the flow of love and separate me from the Light.

TEXT 3- THE AFFIRMATIONS

- I see the Light in the eyes of everyone I meet and recognize them as my True Self.
- I see a teacher in everyone I meet, and I strive to learn the lesson about myself without seeking to give the other person a lesson.
- Each day, my relationships are becoming more peaceful, more loving, and more fun.
- I discover my enlightened self by seeing the enlightened self in others.
- I accept myself, and my life unconditionally.
- I am melting the boundaries of my limited identity and merging with all of creation.
- I am holding my mind in silent readiness to receive the gift of love.

Choose one of the above affirmations and repeat it as often as possible during the day. Set the intention of making the spiritual Truth contained in the affirmation change your experience of life.

The Perception of Truth

The Truth is true. That's the only lesson you have to learn, but it's also the hardest since nothing you currently think to be the Truth is true. Moreover, it's impossible for you to see your error because your perception is distorted.

Distorted Perception

Perception is a mirror. It is your state of mind projected outward, and so what you see reflects what you think. Since your mind is confused, your perception is also confused, and that produces fear and agitation. True perception, on the other hand, fosters love and tranquility.

Your perception is distorted because you bring the past into the present. Your beliefs, which are a distillation of past experiences, limit what you see in the present. And because belief-based perception resists reality, it also wears you out. There's no strain when you see through the eyes of your True Nature which means that you perceive the Truth.

Relinquishing Beliefs

> *"I do have to admit that my life is at times quite a strain."*

Your life is a struggle because you were not created for the environment you made, and therefore you cannot adapt to it. Truth is the only environment in which you will not experience strain because it is the only environment that's consistent with your nature, one that is made in your True Self's image and likeness and imbued with Spirit. You are the thinker of your thoughts, which create your beliefs, which create your reality. Your beliefs will not be taken from you, but they can be given up by you. The choice is yours. You can use your free will to dismantle your belief system and allow true knowledge to appear. Once you undergo this radical shift in your perception, you no longer react out of false understanding and instead act out of true understanding, which comes from the Light. When you rest in the Light, your struggle ends.

"How do I rest in the Light?"

Remember the Truth of who you are. Until now, you've been judging experience, and this has wrapped your mind in a cloak of self-deception (because judgment without deception is impossible). To judge is to lack honesty, and yet honesty is required in order to know the Truth. Honesty means consistency, in which no thought opposes any other thought. Can you, then, observe life without judgment and conflict, and thus see it truly? If you choose to be deceived, you agree to operate with two opposing thought systems, one you made and one that has been given to you. Both cannot be true. The one you choose determines what you see: either a world of Light, wisdom, and peace or a world of darkness, ignorance, and agitation. The Truth does not change. The Light created you to be whole and therefore you are eternally whole. Remain rooted and established in what you truly are. When you get angry or experience any negative feeling, you've fallen into a dream. Wake up and know your True Nature and your true Source. Wake up and remember the Truth.

Dropping Your Identification with the Body

"But I can't pretend that life's wonderful when it clearly isn't. I mean, look at the misery so many people are in."

Don't get distracted by other people. Yes, there are many suffering people in the world, who are suffering because they are lost in an illusion. But how are you to help them if you're lost in an illusion as well? Put on your own oxygen mask before leaning over and helping your fellow passenger.

"And that means doing what?"

Stop perceiving your frail physical body as your source of strength. This is a misperception. You need a body in order to experience this physical world, and so the body is a precious vehicle that should be appreciated and cared for; however, identifying with it is a fundamental error that leads to suffering and fear. Discover your Source and take up residence there. It's time to emerge from deepest mourning into perfect joy. Nothing external will ever satisfy you or make you feel safe because nothing in the world of form lasts.

Every decision you make brings you either sorrow or joy. Sorrow is an inaccurate perception. Correct your perception and so transcend time and live in the timeless present, in which every experience is fresh, alive, and filled with joy. You'll still have a body that will be subject to the passage of time, but you'll be living in eternity. You'll be "in the world but not of it." Outside of time, your mind returns to its natural state of being, which is unconditional love. Perceive the Truth of who you are and you'll discover you're a being that's not born, does not grow old or die, and does not suffer. When you drop your fixation with the physical body and instead perceive your eternal nature, you will see your true self. Then you will naturally and effectively help others because that's what your True Nature does. It shares unconditional love.

The Impossibility of Escape

"Why is it apparently so hard to find the Truth?"

Every action you take to find the Truth fails because you're looking for Truth inside an illusion. You're seeking the Source of Life while living in a mirage. Since you can see pools, rain, and other forms of water, you're convinced that it's only a question of time before you discover the source from which the water arises. However, the Source is real and therefore it can only be found in reality, not in a mirage.

If you accept that you're living in a mirage and react by trying to escape, your efforts are doomed from the outset because you don't know what you need to know in order to achieve this. If you did have true knowledge, you wouldn't be in the mirage in the first place. The more you try to escape from the illusion, the deeper you sink into it, because your attempt at escape is a form of confirmation that the illusion is real.

Trust in Guidance

"If there's nothing I can do to see the Truth, what should I do?"

Give up doing anything. Say this prayer, and mean it:

"I cannot distinguish between Truth and illusion, and so I will stop trying to make the distinction. I've been placing my faith in what's untrue, but now I offer my faith to the Light, which can guide me out of deception into the simple Truth."

Your True Self's plan for your awakening is as perfect as yours is fallible, and would teach you nothing except how to be happy. You have to decide whether you want Light or your darkness, knowledge or your ignorance; you can have one but not both, because Truth is union with your True Self and in that union everything unreal must disappear.

Therefore, allow your True Self's will to guide you. If you deny the will of your True Self you are denying yourself because your True Self's will is your True will. How could it be different? Reality is whole. It is one thing, not two. Therefore, the Truth is one thing, whole and indivisible. The Truth is love, and love is what you are.

Full Immersion in Truth

> *"So you're saying it's simple and hard at the same time?"*

It's simple in the sense that nothing is easier than perceiving the Truth. You have to make an effort not to see it! But at the same time, it's extraordinarily difficult because you keep searching for the Truth in the world of form, which means you can never reach it. The outer form is appearance and appearances hid the Truth because they are not reality. Go beyond the form and you will see the Truth clearly in everything you look upon. The Truth is not hidden from you. It is all around you. You have just been looking in the wrong place.

To See the Truth, Give Up Illusions

> *"What is Truth? And anyway isn't the Truth relative? Doesn't the world already have enough fanatics proclaiming that their Truth is the absolute Truth?"*

Yes, most of what we know as Truth is relative. And, yes, a lot of trouble is caused in the world by people who insist that they know the absolute Truth. But that doesn't mean there is no such thing as fundamental Truth. Consider, for example, the assertion that the world of time and space is an illusion behind which lies a timeless reality. This is not something that is true for certain people in certain circumstances and untrue for other people in other circumstances. There is nothing relative about it whatsoever. And by the way, observe spiritual leaders who genuinely know these kinds of Truths: you won't find them fighting wars, founding cults, or coercing others in any way at all. When you get near to someone who's living in freedom, you experience freedom, not compulsion.

You asked, "What is Truth?" The answer is: Truth is that what does not change. It is the unalterable, unchangeable law, forever and forever. Your True Self is love, and so everything that is love, it's true. Truth is the energy that created you. It's your natural environment. When you stray from that environment, you experience fear—False Evidence Appearing Real. It appears real because the fear originated in an idea that you've made up and thus accept as real, but it isn't real; it's an illusion.

Authentic spiritual teachings urge you to go beyond illusions. In order to let these teachings catalyze your transformation, you have to give them space and allow them to grow and ripen within you. In time they can show you to yourself; show you your original goodness, the hidden treasure that has always been inside you awaiting discovery. When you find this treasure within you, then you will see it within everyone else.

"And to find it, I have to do nothing?"

There's nothing you can do in the normal sense of doing. First, you have to see something, and then you have to not do anything. What you must honestly see is that you are miserable and not happy. At present, you believe your misery is happiness, and while you persist in that mistake, you cannot be taught.

"But I think I am happy!"

If you think you are happy and are not sure whether or not your happiness is real, you can take a simple test. Ask yourself, "Am I completely free of fear?; "Am I always perfectly at peace?" If you cannot answer with an unqualified 'yes' to these questions, and of course you can't, then you are not living the life that your True Self created for *you.* All you need do is recognize this. You don't have to take any action. Of course, it's humbling to admit to yourself that what you had considered to be a perfectly acceptable life is, in fact, Hell. But, that's what you must do because you won't change something that you don't think needs changing. And since your True Self will not force the change on you, you will remain stuck until you allow yourself to see the reality of your situation.

Once you see your life clearly, do nothing; or rather do something that's actually a "not doing": namely, surrender yourself and all your illusions to your True Self. Bring all your dark and secret thoughts to the Light, and look upon them with eyes of love. Your True Self holds the Light, and you are holding the darkness. They cannot exist when both of you together look on them. When your peace is threatened or disturbed in any way, say to yourself, "I do not know what anything, including this, means. And so I do not know how to respond to it. And I will not use my own past learning as the Light to guide me now." Leave room for the Light, and you will find yourself so filled with power that nothing will prevail against your peace.

You see, you can't search for the Truth in your present state of consciousness because all you'll get is more of that consciousness, which is not Truth. You can, however search out everything that interferes with Truth. These are the illusions that you offer up to your True Self.

Connection Inside = Joy Outside

> *"But I really don't have a painful life. I have a great life: lots of friends, a beautiful home, a wonderful family, everything anybody could want. I can't say I don't worry sometimes about falling sick or about what it means to die, but this hardly constitutes living a life of Hell."*

You have to examine this honestly. Do your friends stop you from feeling alone, does your house give you an unshakable sense of being at home, and does your family cause you to experience infinite love? There's nothing to be ashamed about if you answer 'no' to these questions. When you become one with the Truth, you're never lonely, forever at home, and always in a state of unconditional love. In this state, you can go back to your friends, back to your home, and back to your family, and appreciate them truly for the first time. When you try to get fulfillment and love from the outside world, you always suffer, whether you realize it or not; but when you access the true source of love and fulfillment, you are genuinely able to appreciate the world.

Sharing = Receiving

So, admitting that your friends and family don't completely fulfill you is not some form of betrayal. It is, in fact, the beginning of a truly loving relationship with them. When you discover that the Light is within you, you can share it with them. You share your awareness of what you know to be true which causes your awareness of the Truth to deepen. This happens because, since you are one with others, what you give to others you give to yourself. Therefore, the more you share the Truth, the more Truth comes to you. And the more Truth you have to give.

Seek only the Truth. Truth will correct all errors in your mind and you are in need of nothing but the Truth; "No one can fail who seeks to reach the Truth". All you're ever fundamentally searching for is the Truth; therefore, why not upgrade your quest so that it becomes the focus of your life? If it is something that you do only occasionally, when you feel like it, then you have failed to understand Truth's value. Truth is beyond price, for it heals your mind, which makes you whole, which allows you to reconnect with the Light.

The False and the True

> *"I am still having trouble seeing the simplicity in what you're saying."*

You just have to understand this: A loving idea is true; an unloving idea is false. When you judge something, you're having an unloving thought, and thus your judgment is untrue. Therefore, don't judge anything. In the absence of judgment (and the false, unloving ideas that accompany it), Truth and love automatically emerge in you, with no further effort on your part. When true ideas are revealed to you, welcome and embrace them.

When you see the Truth, you will realize that falsehood is impossible. It has not occurred and has had no real effect on you. And in a dream, you just imagine that it was real. But what is untrue today is also untrue in the past, and always will be untrue.

In the two preceding paragraphs, it's been explained in a few words exactly how to tell falsehood from Truth. Here are the instructions again: Your judgments are false; become aware of your judgments and drop them. Why is it so hard to learn such simple things? It has been your decision to make everything natural and easy seem impossible, so that you can maintain the fake comfort of your illusory identity. When you're confronted by a difficult problem you insist on focusing on the form, and thus you bring confusion rather than clarity to the situation. You do this because you're afraid of the unknown and are thus frightened of the Truth, which is the ultimate unknown; you mistakenly believe it may harm you or take something of value from you. What should you do, then? To paraphrase Mother Teresa, feel the fear and step forward anyway into the unknown.

> *"Suppose I break my leg. Am I not supposed to judge that as either good or bad? It certainly doesn't feel good."*

That's true, but the problem is that you're judging the effect, which is the outer form. That's arrogance because you are saying that you understand the entire workings of the universe so perfectly that you perfectly understand the meaning of your broken leg. You don't understand it, and so stop judging it and just observe it. Observe what is going on within you as this situation unfolds in your life. Ask what you are being taught, but don't answer the question. Wait for the question to be answered for you, in whatever way and at whatever time life chooses to give the answer. Have faith that everything is for your good, even your broken leg. Remember that you can't see this from your current time- enmeshed perspective, and so don't try to understand it. Wait patiently for understanding to be brought to you. You don't know what you have to go through in order for your soul to evolve. All you can do is accept whatever comes and be open to it and know that it is an opportunity for growth, and not judge it. That's very hard for you to do because you wake up in the morning and write a fearful script for the day:

> *"I've got too much to do; I don't feel well; I don't know if I can succeed at such and such; I don't know if he/she loves me; If I can get that job, raise, lover, vacation, or home, then I'll be happy; I can't be happy because I don't have a man/woman in my life; I can't be happy because I've got this man/woman in my life; I'm alone; I've got too many things to do; I don't have enough things to do; I don't have a purpose; It's raining; I'm bored because the TV's broken...."*

Fill in the blanks with the details of your own script, and see what you're doing to yourself. Become aware of the scripts you write, and stop writing them.

Don't try changing them to a better script; just drop them completely. When you wake up in the morning, say to your True Self, "I don't know what anything is for and so I hand control over to you, knowing that you will guide me into an ever-deepening experience of love, joy, peace, and Truth." Then, at the end of the day, sit down quietly in meditation, and be grateful for everything that was brought to you, whether you understand its significance or not.

> *"I think there are so many errors in my mind that it's an impossible task for me to bring them all into the Light of awareness."*

Truth corrects all errors. Allow Truth to enter your mind and, whatever the number of errors, they will all vanish, leaving not even a trace by which to be remembered. They are gone because without belief they have no life. A belief is a thought and thoughts create; without the creative energy of thought, an error cannot be sustained. It returns to dust and only Truth remains. So drop your beliefs and accept all that life brings you. Don't resist anything. Everything that's happening is whatever you need to experience in order for your soul to evolve. When you finally perceive the Truth, and you will, all your pain will end. When illusions are gone, there is no longer any fear, doubt, or need for defense. Pain is an illusion, and so your acceptance of the Truth, which is real, erases all the negative conditions in your life.

Want the Truth

> *"This sounds simple while I'm reading it, but afterwards I think back and realize I still don't really understand. Can you make all this as simple as possible for me?"*

Reduced to three words, the essential instruction is this: Want the Truth. That's all.

Want it more than anything else, constantly in every moment. If you really want to perceive the Truth, then you'll willingly drop your preconceived ideas about what kind of life you should live - what you must do, the people you have to associate with, the goals you need to pursue. You'll admit that you really don't know anything. You'll say to yourself, "I am content to go wherever my True Self wishes, knowing that my True Self goes there with me. I do not have to worry about what to say or what to do because my True Self who sent me will direct me."

You are here on Earth to represent the Light, but most of the time you go through life representing an image of yourself that you made up and mistakenly believe to be you. But your thinking is not true thinking; it's an illusion. You know this is so because there is nothing stable in your life. Truth is stable. It does not come and go; it does not shift or change.

> *"I feel that I have been a sincere seeker of Truth all my life and yet I can't honestly say that I have found the Truth. Frankly, I have the impression that I never will."*

When you ask for the Truth, you are asking for something that is already yours. You're asking for something that belongs to you but that you do not yet recognize as your own. Consequently, no one can fail who seeks to reach the Truth. No one—that means you.

At present, failure features prominently in your life because you seek goals that cannot be achieved. You look for permanence in the impermanent, for love where there is none and dream of death. In other words, you keep looking with the bodies' eyes and that is why you don't find the Truth. Instead of seeking the Light, you in effect ask for death, since the pursuit of the imagined leads to nothingness, which is death. You pray for safety and security, but in your heart, you're asking for protection for the tiny, fragile dream you've created.

You are in need of nothing but the Truth. When you dwell in the Truth, all needs are satisfied, all cravings end, all hopes are finally fulfilled, and all dreams vanish. Want the Truth!

Beginner's Mind

> *"If the Truth is always with me, why is it so difficult to see it?"*

Because it is hidden by your selfish desires. This is why you have to remove all the assumptions you have about what you want. These assumptions are based on your perception of appearances instead of reality.

> *"Yes, it's hard not to focus on appearances. When you have no money in your bank account, for example, and your rent needs to be paid and your car payment is late, you're likely to exclaim, "Not look at appearances? How can I not look at the dreadful mess I'm in? I'm going to be evicted next week, and I have nowhere else to go. And even if I did have somewhere to go, I'd have no car to take me there, because in a few days it will be repossessed."*

These are still all appearances and hide the Truth. They deceive you. In actuality, you have everything and are everything, and so there is no such thing as lack. You've just fallen asleep and forgotten who you are. You've let your mind wander off into illusory fear thoughts. Decide to stop that from happening. Absolutely refuse to let your mind slip away. This is why it is so important to spend quiet time with yourself because your True Self instructs only in silence. Its voice will tell you where to go, what to do, whom to speak to, and what to say, and it will also tell you what not to do. There is no separation between you and your True Self: your house, your car, the sheriff who might evict you, and the truck driver who might tow your car. Because of this underlying unity, when your True Self acts, it is able to do so in a whole way that creates perfect outcomes for everyone concerned. To the disconnected mind, Wholeness seems capable of performing miracles, but to the healed mind, it is simply the natural way of thing. You've heard it said that "the Truth will set you free." Now you know why. Truth and illusion cannot coexist, and so the Truth frees you from illusion. Indeed, it's the only freedom there is. Everything else is unreal.

When somebody appears to harm you, realize that what they are doing to the physical body is not the Truth of who they are. Their behavior is presenting to you an opportunity for healing, an opportunity to let go of the judgmental thoughts within your mind. If you are judging the situation, you are seeing with the body's eyes, and that's not True Vision. True vision shows you where to go, whereas judgment gives you false direction. Judgment is a sharp weapon that you use against yourself. You keep using this weapon over and over again, and still, you don't understand why you're hurting. Drop your weapon.

You make a judgment every time you decide what an experience is for. The fact is you don't know the purpose of anything. If you did, you would not experience even one second of fear. Thinking you know the Truth, blocks you from learning the Truth. You cannot be in error and in the Truth at the same time. Therefore, stop thinking you know what you don't know. Cultivate what Zen Buddhism calls the "beginner's mind". Then you can be helped.

Asking for Direction

Imagine you and several friends are driving in unfamiliar territory. You stop and ask a local resident the way, but instead of waiting for his answer you proceed to tell him your desired itinerary, "I'm going to take the road through the forest, across the valley, round the hill, and down by the farm." What's more, all your passengers are simultaneously expressing their own opinions about the best route. Knowing that there's too much of a ruckus going on in your car for him to be heard, the local waits to see if you truly want his answer. However, you've actually forgotten that you even asked a question, and so you drive away before the one person who could give you accurate information has uttered a single word. The car is your mind, the occupants are cacophony that rages in your head, and the local resident is your True Self. And the route through the forest, needless to say, is the wrong one.

Your True Nature is Innocence

To be receptive to your True Self's directions, you have to realize you are guiltless. If you believe you are guilty, you believe you are in error, and this belief stops you from the realization of your Wholeness. Guilt is of the ego, whereas innocence is of your True Nature. Guilt makes you feel undeserving, and so it blocks you from accepting what is rightfully yours.

The good news is that you don't have to decide whether you are innocent or guilty, whether you deserve the Truth or not. Leave that up to your True Self, who knows that you are worthy. Your job is simply to decide that you will no longer try to decide. Then, all decisions become as easy and as right as breathing. There is no effort, and you will be led as gently as if you were being carried down a quiet path in summer. You cannot understand how much your True Self loves you for there is no parallel in your experience of the world to help you understand it.

The Truth is eager to manifest in your life; it wants that above all things. When you seek the Truth as earnestly as it is seeking you, then you will be instantly reunited with it.

Practice

1) Do your daily meditation.
2) At the end of your meditation period, begin your affirmation session.

TEXT 1 -THE SETTING

Take a deep breath, relax, and align yourself with your breathing. Listen to your breath as it flows in and out of your body. Now visualize yourself entering a pyramid. This is your secret sanctuary, and it is filled with stillness and peace. You sit down on a beautiful throne that is the perfect design for you, and perfectly comfortable.

The only energies in this pyramid are your own inner energies. You are completely protected from the external world.

TEXT 2- THE INVOCATION

I invoke the energy of all the angels, archangels and masters. I call on the violet flame to consume, dissolve and purify all my dense thoughts and emotions. I ask for the release of any tendency to be attached, for my attachments are what inhibits the flow of love and separate me from the Light.

TEXT 3- THE AFFIRMATIONS

- I am polishing the mirror of my mind each day.
- I am feasting on the Truth.
- My True Self sees all things as pure.
- I see the current of life flowing behind all forms.
- I see my reflection in everyone.
- My worth is established by my True Self.
- I am here to experience the deliciousness of life by removing everything that blocks my perception of love.
- I experience the bliss and satisfaction that comes from my union with the divine.
- I am healing the ills of my mind with the medicine of Truth.
- I am overflowing with gratitude to be in a physical form at this moment in time.
- I am experiencing more of what I am and less of what I've made.
- I am a pulsating being of Light, radiating through the body.
- I am keeping my fire burning through daily practice.
- My humble efforts are fruitful.
- I am letting go of my limited desires and my limited existence.

Choose one of the above and set the intention of making the spiritual Truth contained in the affirmation change your experience of life.

Claiming Your True Thoughts

The entire universe is thought energy. Since energy is neither created nor destroyed, thoughts are not born and cannot die. Thought energy is natural power that governs the molecular structure of all manifestations, and so thoughts rule creation. They are vibrations, which begin in the mind of the thinker and then extend outward into manifestation.

Thoughts Create

Your True thoughts create universes, whereas your self-made thoughts create your personal reality. You cannot organize your life without a thought system. You develop it, live by it, and teach it (since teaching comes from the example that you give others). Your acceptance of your thought-created reality makes it real. Even if what you're accepting is still in invisible form, it is yours and it will begin moving into the visible world.

Watch Your Thoughts

Therefore it behooves you to become watchful about what thoughts you entertain because they will determine what you experience. Positive thoughts are slow, sound, clear, deep and well directed. Negative thoughts are fast and chaotic. A racing mind is sick; it has no time to finish a thought, much less check on the quality of the thought. A slow mind, on the other hand, is sound and kind; it leaves room for love, tenderness, and compassion. But a still mind is nothing less than divine; it knows its real thoughts and allows unconditional love to flow through it.

Your True Self's Thoughts of You

Your True thoughts include a thought of you that never changes. It is surrounded by stillness so complete no sound of battle comes even close. It rests in certainty and perfect peace. The true thoughts have never left the mind of its Creator, and it never will because your true thoughts are eternal. It exists right now in this instant; it is who you truly are in this present moment. It is your reality. Though you are one, you experience yourself as two on account of the duality created by the small mind. Sometimes you are aware of it and sometimes you are not. The Truth is that you don't have two realities, but one. How could your reality be a thing apart from you, existing in a different world that you know nothing about? There is only one you, outside of which nothing is real.

Your Time is Now

> *"Things aren't going great in my life right now, so I hope that what I'm experiencing, which seems totally real, isn't the one reality of which you speak."*

What's not real is a dream, not an alternative reality. You're living in a dream that seems so real you can't believe it's an illusion. Waking up from the dream is simple, but at the same time challenging. If detecting the illusion were easy, mankind would not have spent the whole of its history acting as if illusions were real. But don't despair; the fact that you're reading this book and perhaps other texts means that you're waking up. Keep going. You're not alone; love is guiding you constantly, whether you're aware of it or not. Your day has come—seize it.

It's time to exchange your mistakes for wisdom so that your errors can serve as catalysts. Nothing's keeping you stuck except your refusal to admit that you might be in error. Denial is the mortal enemy of spiritual progress. If you deny that your house is sinking into quicksand, then it will continue to sink and there's nothing you can do about it, since no one's going to force you to rebuild on a solid foundation. The first step in all aspects of your spiritual growth, therefore, is to see error as error, to realize that the illusion is an illusion, to reveal the false as the false.

The power of decision is your own. You cannot suffer loss unless you decide to. You cannot experience pain unless you choose it. You cannot grieve, be afraid, or think you're sick unless these are the outcomes you unconsciously want. You do not even die without giving your consent. Nothing happens that doesn't represent your deepest wishes, and nothing fails to occur that you have chosen.

Become Acquainted with Your True Self

You can choose differently. The power to reach up, develop, expand, and grow is within you. Look inside and get to know your real thoughts. When you access your real thoughts, they will dissolve the man-made fearful thoughts that are confining you. Pure thoughts convey goodness, kindness, thoughtfulness, meaningfulness, and sharing, whereas impure thoughts bring only upset into your Mind.

You are too blessed to be stressed. Let go of any emotion that is fueled by the past; it only creates commotion, which is a signal that you are out of balance and your energy is being blocked by a belief system. Remove the block and allow the flow of pure energy to resume. Let go of your mistaken identity and accept yourself as you were created. That is the only you that the True Self knows. Everything has already been decided for you by the Universal Mind. You cannot undo your True Self's will, and so why not just accept it? Accept your True Self because who you think you are does not change the Truth of who you really are.

> *"No disrespect intended, but I don't like the idea that everything is fixed by Universal Mind. What happened to free will?"*

You ask the question because you don't yet understand the beauty of Wholeness, in which your will is one with Universal Mind. In the world of duality, your free will means doing something that's independent of your True Self. In the instant of Wholeness, your will is the will of your True Self. There's no separation and therefore no sense that something is being imposed on you.

The View from 30,000 Feet

All spiritual texts teach that you don't understand the meaning of anything because, in your separated state, you don't see the whole picture. You judge events from the viewpoint of your small, separated mind, which means you understand nothing.

Life is full of examples demonstrating that the big picture is radically different than the small one. In California, there's a marvelous natural phenomenon: wildfires. Yes, that's a controversial statement, given that every year in this part of the world forest fires destroy homes and kill people. Most of these fires are of human origin, set either by careless campers or amoral arsonists. However, there are also natural fires, usually caused by Lightning, and their role in the ecology of the Californian forests is fascinating. In fact, one of the grandest and the most beautiful creations, the giant Sequoia, depends on fire for its existence.

Across the Sierra Nevada mountain range, sprinklings of giant Sequoias rise out of the pine, creating a breathtaking sight; as they are the most massive living things on earth. They dwarf every other tree in the forest. Their trunks are so broad you can carve a tunnel in one of them and drive a car through it (and California being the tourist-minded state that it is, has indeed welcomed it). Hundreds of feet up in the air, the trunk is topped by a mop of branches and leaves; amongst this foliage hang tiny cones containing minuscule seeds. The question is: How does the tree reproduce? In its natural environment, the surrounding ground is covered by a carpet of dead and decaying twigs and branches. How do the seeds reach the soil and take root? The answer is that the giant Sequoia stands there waiting patiently until a forest fire passes through. The flames do not harm the tree, which contains an anti-inflammable compound (giving the trunk its characteristic red hue), but they consume the deadwood. As a result of this conflagration, a layer of ash is created that contains vital nutrients required for the seeds' growth. The heat rising up from the flames causes the cones, which may have remained closed for centuries, to open, sending a shower of seeds down to the newly prepared earth. Seen in this broader perspective, a disaster (the wildfire) can be understood as a blessing.

Though the wonders of nature are insignificant in comparison with the wonders of Heaven, the different realms of the universe reflect one another, and so the perfection that is seen in nature resembles the exquisite perfection that exists in Universal Mind. When your True Self's thoughts are yours, you will see with eyes of love, and you will realize that everything, without exception, is exactly the way it is supposed to. The world will never look the same you again.

Want to Change

> *"I'm prepared to accept that I don't see the whole picture and am living in a dream, but what do I do in order to wake up?"*

Absolutely refuse to let yourself slip out of the constant awareness of what is happening in your mind. Watch the continual stream of thoughts as it passes through and, when you perceive an unloving thought, resolutely refuse to give it any attention. Thoughts feed on attention and they wither when deprived of it. Withdraw your attention from unloving thoughts and create space for loving thoughts, such as, "I am whole as my True Self is whole; Wholeness created me as a whole being."

Everything arises from your thoughts: your words, actions, decisions, desires, and destiny. Every decision you make stems from your idea about who you are and the value you put upon yourself. Your self-value is a mental judgment that originates in your separated mind. If your mind were whole and you were thinking your true real thoughts, you would not be judging yourself the way you do. Do you realize you are always judging yourself? Every time you say "I'm sad" or "I'm happy" or "I'm a mother" or "I'm a doctor," you're attaching a label to yourself, and that's a judgment. You feel compelled to justify and explain everything, rather than allowing yourself and your experiences to simply be what they are, without any story attached. You have to decide who you are going to serve—your True Self or the False Self. Serving your True Self means to see yourself as your True Self sees you. And in order to do that, you have to be aware of what is going on within your mind—your likes, dislikes, opinions, and so on. See them, but don't attach any meaning to them, otherwise you're adding one more judgment onto your existing judgments, all of which are unreal.

You have to let go of everything artificial and value only what is real. Only Love is real. You can make a decision to end the separation and get to know your True Self, as your True Self knows you. Or, you can stay as you are. But you can't serve two masters. You can't want to change and also want to cling to your false beliefs. That would be like asking for directions out of the jungle and then ignoring them, continuing down the path that got you lost in the first place.

In other words, you have to make a decision: Are you going to listen to the "still small voice" within you (your real thoughts) or are you going to continue to make your own thoughts? Nothing happens until you make the decision in favor of your True Self. You have to declare, and mean it truly from your heart, that you want to change. In order to change, you have to learn to think differently. You do this by seeing the pain that your current thinking is causing you. For as long as you're complacent about your life, you'll see no reason to change it. Therefore, you have to come out of denial and take stock of your current experience. Are you really going to continue believing that your self-created reality is true reality? And if you break through this belief, and realize that your True Self would never give you the experiences you're having, are you then going to substitute a new belief and tell yourself that your life will improve in the future, perhaps after you die? The "Now" is all there is, and so if you want to have your real thoughts, choose them now. Become fed up with what you're experiencing and want a new life more than you've ever wanted anything before.

Use everything that happens to you for your awakening. Every single instant is an opportunity for you to wake up and become more aware of who you really are.

Who are you? You're an eternal being whose nature is love, Light, and joy.

Choose Loving Thoughts

> *"I wish I could believe that. At present, I seem to be having more than my fair share of darkness."*

Your destructive thoughts have been generating destructive behavior and actions. Choose constructive thoughts and your behavior and actions will become constructive. Destructive thoughts bring fear, whereas constructive thoughts bring joy. Constructive thoughts are your real thoughts.

When you are not aware of your True thoughts, you become dejected, and then you dream external things into existence that can lift you up. As a result, you seek satisfaction in the "four P's": Power, Profit, Prestige, and Pleasure. But the fulfillment you long for never comes.

Fulfillment is an aspect of unconditional Love and if you are to experience it, you must allow your thoughts to be corrected. Your destructive thoughts bring you a life that is dull, shallow, scattered and confused, whereas your real thoughts bring you eternal joy. They are healing agents that will restore reality to you. When you merge with your real thoughts, they will carry you like a river, freely, effortlessly, and bountifully. At present, you live in a world of cause and effect, but in love there is no cause and effect. Love simply is. Your True Self is an energy field of love that is everywhere and in everything. Wherever you are, your True Self is; there is nowhere you can be without your True Self. Everything is love and everything must end in love. So, decide now to choose loving thoughts.

Spiritual Law

> *"I still don't understand why I'm in this dream that I can't wake up from. It seems as if the universe is cruel and punishing."*

Nothing that happens to you is a punishment. When you foolishly jump off a wall and break your leg, you don't blame gravity; you accept that you violated a law. The same is true in the invisible world. You're violating spiritual principles constantly, but you don't see what you're doing. One such law is that what you send out comes back to you. If you throw a bouncy ball against your living room wall, you are not surprised that its trajectory causes it to come back and smack you on the forehead. Likewise, when you throw anger, resentment, or judgment at other people it can come back and hurt you.

For one thing, you get the immediate experience of those unpleasant feelings. And in addition, because you live in a reflective world, you cause other people to throw anger, resentment, or judgment around, meaning that even more unpleasantness bounces back at you. When this happens, don't blame life. It's providing valuable feedback about spiritual laws and giving you an opportunity for you to become more patient, tolerant and unconditionally loving. Use the information to stop acting in ways that are similar to jumping off high walls or bouncing balls in confined spaces.

Again, in order to change what you experience, your thoughts must be corrected. Until they are, your life will remain dull, scattered, and confused, for nothing of value grows in shallow soil. Thoughts share the attributes of their creator.

The thoughts you think are in your small mind as you are in the Universal Mind which thought of you. You've forgotten the thought Universal Mind holds of you, but that thought is perfectly unchanged by your forgetting. Like immutable stars in an eternal sky, your true thoughts are far beyond all change and shine forever. They wait for you to remember and welcome them.

"Which thought the Universal Mind does have of me?"

The thought Universal Mind holds of you is your uncontaminated nature, the truth about who you are: Love. Only love is real, therefore, your reality must be a reality of love.

All true thoughts are loving and so, if what you're thinking is not a loving thought, it is not a true thought; stand guard at the door of your mind and monitor your thoughts. Shakespeare wrote, "All things are ready if the mind be so." Ask yourself, "What can I do to access my real loving thoughts right now?" From loving thoughts, loving words and actions will follow. Knowledge is the recognition of what is real; therefore, to know the Truth one must make it real by living it in thought, word, and action.

Commitment

"Put that way, it sounds simple."

It is simple. But you need to commit to your own awakening. Your thinking will remain erratic until you make a firm commitment to listen to your real thoughts. Commitment transforms dreams into reality. Until one is committed, there is hesitancy, there is the chance to draw back, which always take to ineffectiveness. Concerning all acts of initiative (and Creation), there is one elementary Truth—the ignorance of which kills countless ideas and splendid plans. The moment one definitely commits oneself, then providence moves too. All thoughts of things occur that would never otherwise have occurred. A whole stream of events issues from the decision, raising in one's favor all manner of unforeseen incidents and meetings and material assistance, which no man could have dreamed would come his way. As Johann Wolfgang von Goethe reminds us, "Whatever you can do, or dream you can, begin it. Boldness has Genius, Power, and Magic in it."

> *"I'm ready to make a commitment to monitoring my thoughts, but it seems such a monumental task—there are so many of them. Should I start with the big thoughts and leave the little ones to take care of themselves?"*

There is no such thing as a little thought. The fact that it's a thought means it needs to be well directed. Your True Self's world is nothing but thought, but real thoughts can only be heard when the mind is still. In quietness, you receive the loving thoughts. Simply do this: lay aside all ideas about what you are and what love is. Empty your mind from all images you hold about yourself: everything true or false, good or bad, right or wrong. Hold onto nothing. In that emptiness, your True Self will fill you, for it is the function of your True Self to govern its creation. The world you see does nothing for you and holds nothing that you want. It merely represents your thoughts. Beyond this world is a world you want. It is impossible to see the two worlds at the same time, but when you decide to change your mind, the world will automatically transform. Your new life will be a continuous expression of sublime love, in which you understand that love is the only Master.

Who do you want to serve? the selfish will or the Selfless Will? The choice is yours. Say to your True Self, "Decide for me. My mind is nothing, but my Mind is everything. Help me dissolve my mind so that my true Light may shine." Don't berate yourself for being stuck in the mind. Self-criticism is another of the mind's creations. Instead of feeding on guilt and shame, allow your real thoughts to be your daily bread.

Opening the Channel

Remember, it is not your task to search for love but to allow love to flow through you by opening a channel for it. Be a clear and open channel. Let your thoughts be wholesome and pure allowing no impure thoughts to pollute your mind. The forms of your experience don't matter; only your thoughts that are behind the form do.

The thought is more powerful than the thing itself.

Changing Your World

You are addicted to your self-made thoughts, which deplete your energy. Are you tired of being trapped in a world of pain, suffering, despair, depression, deprivation, distress, effort, loneliness and grief? Are you ready and willing to have your delusional beliefs and attitudes exposed? Are you willing to let go of all that you have made and discover that you are eternally supported by the Universe?

To find out if you are making spiritual progress, ask yourself, "Am I at peace? Am I more tolerant, less judgmental, and more loving?" If what you are doing gives you peace, the thought behind your action is a loving thought. If what you're doing makes you anxious, the thought behind your action is a self-made thought. When your thoughts are keeping you stuck in the illusion of separation, extricate yourself by asking, "What do I want: peace or conflict?" Then choose peace.

Abandon all illusions and reside in the Temple of Bliss. You are moving from a lower to a higher, more complete level of reality—from separated fear consciousness and reaction to unified love consciousness and action. You are emerging from an illusion of what you think you are to the acceptance of what you actually are. Be present now. Just be. Being is the language of the soul. Do not compromise or adjust, for adjustment of any kind are of the ego. Remove the veils that are clouding your awareness of the presence of love. Realize that love is always present; it is you who are absent. This is because you are more concerned about things outside you that deplete your energy and create the illusion of aloneness than you are about Truth, which fulfills you. Stop lamenting the past and planning the future. The mind engaged in planning is not allowing for change, and that leads to suffering.

The Reflective World

> *"Are you saying that if I change, the world my experience will also change?"*

Exactly. The world is not separate from you, any more than your image in the mirror is independent of you. If you looked in the mirror and saw an emaciated body, you wouldn't blame your reflection. You'd feed the body, not try to stuff food into its image.

The material world is how the Light manifests itself to you in countless forms. Whatever is manifesting in your life right now is affected by how you receive it. If you feel detestable, hatred will appear. If you feel lovable, then love will appear. Your True Self can give you only as much love as you are open to receiving. Total acceptance allows love to flow without interruption. Love operates according to the law of attraction, and when you use the law of Love correctly, everything you desire comes into manifestation. Loving thoughts allow your good to come forth attracting the substance to you like a magnet.

All you have to do is to let go of the results conceived by your personality so that the magnificent outcome conceived by your True Self may emerge.

Dissolving the Blocks

Doubt destroys this outcome, whereas trust ensures it. When you confidently accept what is, then every moment is the best possible moment for you. Your pre-occupation with results, makes you tense, anxious, and exhausted, for ego-driven activity depletes your energy. Your trust in a loving outcome, on the other hand, enables you to work peacefully, without agitation or tension.

When you trust, you are naturally patient. Patience arises from your confident awareness that your True Self is the doer. Patience attains the goal. Therefore, wait patiently for Light's bounty to be borne to you on wings of love. Be gentle with yourself. Your True Self's thoughts are meaningful and they will ultimately manifest in a way that is the best outcome for you and the world. Your True Self created a meaningful world, and when you align with your real thoughts, you create a meaningful world, too.

> *"In my experience, the world is both ugly and beautiful; depending on which direction you look. I don't understand how anybody could see it differently."*

That's because you're looking at the world in time. True beauty is a state of being that transcends time and form. It is unlimited, eternal, and formless. Time is a belief of the ego whereas eternity is an idea of your True Self. The world as you know it will end when your thoughts become real. Are you willing to risk such a radical shift? Are you willing to open your mind to receive the gifts that are waiting for you? Do you wish to bring the false self to an end, to die daily to the personality self? The term "personality" comes from the Latin word "persona," meaning mask. Are you willing to remove the mask, end the past, and experience something unimaginably new?

What blocks you is lack of love, identification with a superficial self, and identification with time. But the past is gone, so let it go, and the future is imaginary, so give no thought to it. Your problems are not caused by anything that happened in the past or anything that might happen in the future; they are caused by your decision to leave the reality of the present and wander in the imaginary realm of time. But the past is over and the future doesn't exist, and so neither one can harm you unless you dream that it can. Come back to the present, in which there is only joy. Let everything that is blocking you dissolve.

Where there is joy, there is also love, for they are identical. Your consciousness is like a radio that can be tuned either to the lower frequency thoughts of fear or to the higher frequency thoughts of love. Watch your mind and tune into the frequency of love and joy. Are you willing to accept the higher vibration of energy that is being extended to you, and allow your soul to steer you? If so, you need to withdraw your ego projections and instead look within. Step out of the raging waters of "me, mine and more" and enter the tranquil waters of pure love. Drop arrogance.

"I would love to have true love in my life."

And you can have it. You already do have it, in fact, but you've forgotten that you do. The essence of everything you desire is inside you, but you fail to recognize it. You have unwisely invested in time and human destiny, and the dividend has been a self-created image that gives you false direction and makes extravagant demands on you. Invest instead in your internal goals of self-acceptance, harmony, peace, joy, creativity, and self-knowledge. The dividend will be your true inheritance.

If love is in short supply for you, it is not on account of lack of love in your past, it is because you are not extending love in the present. Your choice to judge rather than to know is the reason you lack peace and love in your life. If you judge, you cannot love.

When you see yourself in the Light, you do not judge because you don't know what anything is for. You just observe it without attaching any meaning to it, allowing the Light within you to interpret it for you. Arrogance tells you that you know what an event is for, which makes you blind, whereas humility opens your eyes so that you may see with single vision.

An arrogant person blocks the Truth because he's afraid of it, whereas a humble person welcomes the Truth because he has faith in it. He does not claim to know what anything is for and instead allows the Light to interpret events on his behalf. His mind is quiet and filled with thoughts of Wholeness. His heart is filled with certainty and peace.

Practice

1) Do your daily meditation.
2) At the end of your meditation period, begin your affirmation session.

TEXT 1 - THE SETTING

Take a deep breath, relax, and align yourself with your breathing. Listen to your breath as it flows in and out of your body. Now visualize yourself entering a pyramid. This is your secret sanctuary, and it is filled with stillness and peace. You sit down on a beautiful throne that is the perfect design for you, and perfectly comfortable. The only energies in this pyramid are your own inner energies. You are completely protected from the external world.

TEXT 2- THE INVOCATION

I invoke the energy of all the angels, archangels and masters. I call on the violet flame to consume, dissolve and purify all my dense thoughts and emotions. I ask for the release of any tendency to be attached, for my attachments inhibit the flow of love and separate me from the Light.

TEXT 3- THE AFFIRMATIONS

- I surrender my thoughts to the Light.
- I rest in the Light. I am floating in the river of life, easily and gracefully.
- I am partaking of the mystical joys of life.
- The Light descends on me and I am purified and blessed.
- I am filled with a sense of my original identity.
- I breathe the divine breath.
- I am living in my natural environment.
- My inner faculties are developed and expanding.
- I am living and working with supreme confidence.
- My gentle approach to life is my strength.
- I am drinking at the fountain of wisdom.

- I am giving the highest expression of myself in everything I undertake.
- I am the knowing principle in all things.

Choose one of the above affirmations and repeat it as often as possible during the day.

Effortless Prosperity

You were born out of abundance into abundance. You are a part of the whole, made in the image of love, and because of this, you lack nothing. Do you imagine your True Self is lacking in any area, whether it be resources, love, joy, or any other expression of abundance? Of course not. Gaze at the star-filled sky on a clear night, breathe in the fragrance of an exquisite flower garden, watch the rain falling, and listen to innocent children singing in the fields: if you drop your mind-forged ideas of poverty, can you see anything to contradict the self-evident Truth that an unlimited nature created this Universe?

Your Natural Prosperity

> *"But we've been taught that the desire for money is not spiritual. How can we become both prosperous and enlightened?"*

You don't become prosperous and enlightened, because you already have these attributes. Your real nature is prosperity and enLightenment itself, and therefore the idea that you lack anything is an illusion. Your small self believes in lack, and because you're identified with this self, you believe in lack too.

Remember the universe mirrors your beliefs to you, and so your mistake appears real. The Truth is that you are an extension of source energy and this means that you are a conduit for infinite possibilities. Because the source contains everything that ever was or ever will be.

True Abundance

In the world of illusions, we measure success solely by external achievements and give exaggerated importance to our possessions and the state of our finances. But there's far more to abundance than money. You may or may not have a high net worth, but if you are rich in spirit, you have all the wealth your heart could ever desire. Abundance knows that anything is possible at any time. Abundance is being aligned with an unlimited force that is working for the highest good of every living thing. If Life's purposes require $10 billion to flow through you, $10 billion will flow through you, and nothing in this world will be able to stop it. But if a materially simple life is what furthers the sublime aims of the Truth, then a materially simple life is what you will have. If you're working for the Light, this will not make the slightest bit of difference to you because you'll know that true abundance has nothing to do with the amount of money you have in your bank account. When you are fully connected to the Source, everything is provided to you in the perfect way at the perfect time and you know it. That's wealth.

Releasing Your Prosperity

> *"I've been working with prosperity ideas for decades, and I'm still struggling materially. What am I doing wrong?"*

Abundance is ready to pour out of you, and the only reason it doesn't is because you block it. Your self-created mind is built of negative beliefs, including those that keep you stuck in the illusion of lack. This belief system is like a sluice that controls the flow of water: an attitude of prosperity opens the gate, while poverty consciousness shuts it. When you let your small self dissolve, your True Self emerges, and you discover that your nature is abundant.

Abundance, therefore, flows from the inside out. There must be an in-working of prosperous ideas before there can be an out-working of prosperous results. When you think affluently, you begin to demonstrate affluence. Affluence does not just mean having things, it means free flow; so, as you apply spiritual principles to your life, you recognize that the free flow of substance can only come from within. You have free will, and therefore have the power to keep your good from flowing. But then why would you do that?

> *"That's a good question. Where did my poverty consciousness come from and why is it still dominating my life?"*

You have absorbed various beliefs from your family and society, and, though you are aware of your underlying sense of poverty, you're not conscious of the specific beliefs that block you from the material abundance that would otherwise come to you. In other words, the reason you have not successfully applied prosperity principles in the past is that you have not brought your negative beliefs into the Light of your awareness. You've created an overlay of positive thoughts, but behind them, the same old ideas of lack are operating, and they are creating your reality. Because you don't see these ideas, you say to yourself, "Well, I've been thinking positively for three months and nothing's changed." That's because you haven't really changed.

> *"How do I change? How do I unlock the door leading to my prosperity?"*

The Gratitude Key

Apply the gratitude principles that you learned in Chapter Four. When you become truly grateful, one of the consequences is that you connect to the divine law of multiplication. Anything you have that you are thankful for will be increased. This is because where attention goes, energy flows, and since you live in a reflective universe that returns what you send out, if you see the value of every moment, ever-increasing value will come back to you. As we've seen, if this natural flow of energy is blocked in you, it's because your mind is enmeshed in mistaken ideas of lack and limitation. The mechanism of the universe is such that it mirrors back confirmation of your poverty-based beliefs.

The Acceptance Key

So, the question to ask yourself is whether you can quietly accept what is. Can you accept the Truth about yourself? You are the rich child of a loving creator. The universe is flowing through you, and therefore you are by nature abundant. If you fail to draw to you what is rightfully yours, then your thoughts must not be the thoughts you were created to think. When you come from love, you receive more love, which is the true substance of abundance; when you come from fear, you get more of what makes you afraid. Observe the results of your beliefs, take responsibility for what you're experiencing, and choose again differently.

The Feeling Key

Negative thinking produces negative feelings; so, when you're feeling low, observe your thoughts and notice what they're telling you. The thoughts are lies, whereas the awareness that observes them is an aspect of your higher self that knows the Truth. Therefore, your awareness of the thoughts tells you the Truth about them. The problem is that you've become so comfortable in your discomfort that you'd rather be stuck than open yourself to something new. But if you are determined to perceive the Truth of your infinite potential, your belief in lack will spontaneously dissolve.

The Decision Key

Everyone can do this. It requires deciding, once and for all, that you're going to take charge of your life. Prosperity is a natural consequence of this decision. Prosperity includes peace of mind, harmony, health, and wealth. True prosperity does not depend upon a full pocketbook, but on a mind rich with rich thoughts. The only lack that exists is the thought of lack; we are children of wealth and our success is the most natural thing in the world.

> *"What's my role, then, in creating prosperity?"*

Your role is to sow the seeds. You have the same relationship with the universe as a gardener has to his garden. The seeds already exist; your job is to plant them in the correct soil and expose them to the right amount of sunshine and rain.

Apart from this, the process is automatic. Pear seeds grow into pears, orange seeds grow into oranges, and Light seeds grow into Light. The Light seed is within each of us, but it must be nurtured and allowed to grow through the practice of spiritual discipline.

The Non-Attachment Key

> *"You say we can be wealthy, but many rich people are unhappy. And also, many rich people use their money in a way that harms others and harms the planet. Indeed, the Bible itself tells us that 'money is the root of all evil.' Surely, then, it's unwise to seek material wealth."*

Look back at the Bible and you will see that you have made a common mistake and quoted the phrase with a key word missing. It is actually written that "the love of money is the root of all evil" (1 Timothy 6:10 KJV). Understand love in this context to mean attachment and you have a profound Truth about prosperity: there is nothing wrong with prosperity itself, only with your demands (attachments) about it. The more attached you are to outer material success, the poorer you are inward, because your attachment means you are unaware of your infinite nature. Unfortunately, in today's world, most people sport their outer riches while remaining empty inside. Their lives trundle along a rut made of concepts and assumptions that keep them in lack and limitation.

Unless you embark on the voyage of self-discovery, you will stay stuck in the illusion of your inner poverty, and as a result, you will always misuse outer wealth. According to his biography, Howard Hughes, the famous aviation pioneer, is a case in point; a man with immense external resources, he was inwardly lonely, miserable, and tortured. As a result, he used his wealth to bully and control others, and in the process his life turned into a tragedy.

However, just because there are countless examples of rich men (and, to a lesser extent, women) who have indulged their acquisitiveness and greed at the expense of others, it doesn't mean that you, in this age of rapidly evolving consciousness, must do the same thing. If you harbor a fear of lack in your heart, you will act in a greedy, selfish way whether you have money or not. So, concentrate on purifying yourself of your fear of lack, and then your actions will be pure regardless of your financial standing.

> *"But isn't it egotistic to want to have more than your fair share of the pie?"*

Self-realized people want everyone to have all of the pie. They want you to connect with the unlimited success and prosperity that is part of your essential nature. What's more, since your belief in lack originates in the ego, you should realize that there is nothing more egotistic than stubbornly clinging to this belief.

What if you have a divine purpose in your life that involves receiving huge amounts of money? Do you really think that blocking out this possibility is an egoless action? You're supposed to reach your full potential, and you can't do this by limiting yourself.

Money is a form of energy that can be used for good or for evil. Be someone who uses it for good. The spiritual teacher Lanza del Vasto used to give this analogy to explain our proper relationship with money: Think of yourself as a bank teller; tens of millions of dollars may pass through your hands in your lifetime, and yet you are not sullied by them. That's because, as a teller, you don't assume ownership of the money and so are not attached to it. Cultivate this attitude toward money and you will never have problems with it. Your money doesn't truly belong to you, for you entered the world penniless, and will leave it that way. In between the two mysterious parentheses created by your birth and death, everything you receive is on loan from your True Self, and so your highest relationship with money is to let it flow through you without sticking and to ensure that you place it in the service of the Light.

The Nature of True Success

> *"If we don't measure success by our external achievements, what is true success, then?"*

Success is knowing yourself truly and living from that place. Success is about being you, right here and right now. It's sharing, it's love, it's the expansion of consciousness, it's living your divine purpose. It has nothing to do with getting anywhere in the future and everything to do with claiming your inner wealth in the here and now.

Several years ago a close friend of mine, Jonathan, spent a month in the beautiful city of Santiago in Chile. His host lived in the city's most elegant neighborhood, across the street from the Santiago Polo Club. The houses and apartment blocks rivaled the most upscale areas of affluent cities like Zurich and Frankfurt. Indeed, so many luxury German automobiles cruised the streets that it was hard to imagine one was not in a wealthy region of Switzerland or Germany. Every morning, he walked along the street bordering the Polo Club, on his way to a 28-day conference in which he was participating. And every morning he walked past a lowly worker whose sole occupation appeared to be to ensure that the sidewalk was free of litter and dog mess and that the islands of grass and flowers were kept in an immaculate condition. The man was in his sixties and must have stood barely five feet high. A soft, almost beatific smile lit up his face. Indeed, his inner radiance lit up the entire street from one end to the other. Jonathan said that you couldn't walk through that field of energy without being uplifted by it. Even the local residents, who had long ago stopped acknowledging the man's existence, must nevertheless have experienced an elevation in consciousness thanks to his presence in their neighborhood. The young heiresses to billion-dollar fortunes, who rode their beautiful mares along a trail running around the polo field, must have become just a little sweeter and a little more loving after passing briefly through the beacon of Light that emanated from this otherwise unremarkable man.

The conference was partly to do with personal success. In his heart of hearts, Jonathan knew that all the attendees needed to do—in order to discover everything they needed to know about success—was to go as a group down to the street by the polo grounds and simply sit in the sidewalk sweeper's energy field. But he never made the suggestion. Nor did he ever talk to him, though he often wanted to. On his last day in Santiago, with a taxi waiting to convey him to the airport, he walked out into the street with the intention of saying goodbye to the saintly sweeper. He wanted to thank him for everything his mere presence had given him during his stay, and he also wanted to give him money, not just to help him, although that was partly his intention, but to acknowledge the value of his contribution to the world, publicly unrecognized though it was. He looked up and down the street, and there was no sign of him. Then he remembered that it was Saturday; he didn't work on weekends.

Though he had missed the opportunity to interact with this inspiring man, his teaching about the nature of success had been communicated to him loud and clear. He was a living example of how successful living depends upon who you are on the inside. If any of the millionaires in that Santiago neighborhood had known what inner bliss that sidewalk sweeper was experiencing and seen the secret impact he was having on the world, they would willingly have given up a part of what they owned to trade places with him.

You have the potential for this kind of true success and no one wants you to give up everything you own to achieve it. But you do need to conduct a rigorous internal inquiry in order for it to develop and become actual.

> *"How does knowing myself lead to success in the outer world? I thought you said that the one thing had nothing to do with the other."*

When you are connected with your True Nature, you discover that you come with genius powers that are factory installed. All the knowledge you need is within you and, when you tap into it, ideas come to you that enable you to do whatever you want to do. When you use your Mind in the right way, you have access to a wealth of ideas. These ideas, and the thoughts of which they are composed, are creative energies that tend to manifest in the world of form. When you dissolve your mind and consciously operate from the Mind, you start to co-create with your Creator; on the other hand, when you identify with the small self and use your mind as a defense against separation, all you'll get are mis-creations.

Aligning with Your True Self

As was mentioned in the last chapter, your thoughts, whether positive or negative, create your reality. All things that are now in form originated as ideas. If your consciousness generates ideas based on separation rather than wholeness, you give birth to wrong ideas that lead to suffering and struggle. If you think you're separate, you believe you have to manipulate the world so that you can make money or acquire things and thus feel better. But when you understand the oneness of life, you realize that your only task is to attain the state of consciousness through which the substance will flow when it is needed. You become like a magnet that draws exactly what is required at exactly the right time. Whether you want a job, relationship, a new home, or money, you first create it as a thought. Where and when it will show up in the world of form, you don't know; but in your mind you know it will manifest and that when it comes you will recognize it.

There was a time in my life when I had to move with my two children out of the house that we'd lived in together for twenty years. It was a hard time for Michael and Ashley who, since they were little, had lived in the house and loved it. They were fearful that our move into the overpriced regions near Los Angeles might mean we'd end up living in a hovel. I knew the right house was waiting for us somewhere, but even though I tried to convey this sense of certainty to Michael and Ashley, I could tell they were not convinced. We followed one lead after another and each time there was something wrong with the place. The children were becoming increasingly despondent. Finally, we saw a house that was halfway decent and Michael was determined that we should take it. "No," I told him, "this is not it. When we see the house that's ours, I'll know it." We carried on searching. One tip led to another tip, and finally we walked into a house, and I said, "This is the place." The children felt the same thing, but then they began to worry that perhaps we were too late, or wouldn't qualify, or wouldn't have the needed references. "All that is taken care of," I reassured them. And it was taken care of, and we moved into the house.

An intelligence is operating for good and all you have to do is align with it and trust it. Follow your desire with no attachment to results, and what you desire will manifest in the right way at the right time. My children have now witnessed the reality of this process.

> *"It's easy to say 'all you have to do is align with the intelligence' but it isn't always so easy to do that."*

If you're not experiencing this alignment right now, that's fine. You're here on the planet to learn, and so you shouldn't be surprised, or get impatient, when you realize that you still have a lot of learning to do. Have compassion for yourself and accept where you are in your life right now. Your True Self has compassion for you and accepts you as you are, so why give yourself anything less? When you reconnect with your essential qualities of compassion and self-acceptance, you become more of who you truly are, and therefore more like your True Self, and therefore more in alignment with the Source that gave you life.

Realize that it is your True Self's function to take care of you and to provide what is needed when, and as it is needed. Your function is merely to recognize that you are one with your True Self. If you have a split mind, with one part focusing on positive thoughts and the other part unconsciously focusing on negative thoughts, then you cannot be a co-creator. When there is no separation in your mind, when you are awake, aware and alive, then you draw the substance to you without effort. All your needs are then filled.

Baby Steps

This is not something that happens overnight. You have to move from a shaky place of belief to a solid place of knowledge, and this comes with experience. The best thing to do is to start with a simple desire that your mind can accept as being realizable. Apply the principle of abundance (which is: set the intention and surrender your attachment) and wait for the outcome with as much confidence as you can muster. The result may not come in the form you expected, but it will come, and you'll say to yourself, "Hey, this process works!" Your trust in the process will gradually strengthen and you will be able to apply it to increasingly ambitious goals. Since the process is an expression of Love, you'll be starting to trust Love. You'll see more and more clearly that you are an aspect of Love and a manifestation of Source energy. You'll realize that you're here to enjoy everything on this planet. As your confidence grows, you'll allow Love to be the director and to show you the way.

Another Look at Attachment

Again, beware of attachment. If you become attached to what you receive from Love, you'll block the process. Imagine you are walking along a beautiful beach in the tropics. Dotted here and there are the loveliest seashells you have ever seen, exquisitely formed and in translucent colors that seem to belong to a different, more ethereal planet. You come across one of these shells, and you're enchanted by it. You must have it, and therefore you pick it up. And so it goes on, with the next shell and the next one. Soon, your hands are so full of shells you cannot pick up any more. You become preoccupied with these shells- not letting any fall off the pile, ensuring none are stolen, and in the end, not only do you not see or enjoy the thousands of other shells on the beach, but you don't get to enjoy the shells you have.

The message in this analogy is: don't hold onto stuff. Let things come to you and don't put up a fight when they depart from you. When you resist the loss of worldly forms, it is because you have made them into false gods and have started to worship them. What else is it but idol-worshipping, when you give over your power to your car, your house, your job, your spouse, your children, or your bank account, allowing them to determine whether you feel fulfilled or not? All these possessions and people are temporary phenomena in your life, and one day they will disappear. And if they don't disappear now, you can be sure they will do so at the time of your death. Entrusting them with your sense of wellbeing is a poor investment that can only lead to disappointment and suffering.

Your Power is Here Now

Realize that nothing real is happening outside. The real action is on the inside, hidden from your physical eyes. When you start to see with inner vision, you understand that you already are what you seek: you are love, you are joy, you are infinite fulfillment. Because you don't see this at present, your mind goes into a state of wanting, taking, and grabbing. You keep looking outside yourself for something that isn't there. Stop searching and look within, into your true nature, where you are already aligned with the laws of abundance.

You have the power right here and now to manifest whatever you desire. Look within and let go of fear thoughts by recognizing that by being who you truly are you automatically have everything you truly need. You have to become so rooted and established within this understanding that it governs everything you do.

Be determined that you will no longer depend upon a person, place, thing or condition for your prosperity. Prosperity is an inner state. It's what you are, and therefore it is your true nature. Since nothing you experience in the external world can add to or subtract from your Wholeness, you no longer need to look outside yourself for fulfillment. From this perspective, getting is meaningless, while giving is the only thing that matters.

> *"I'd like to believe I have the power to manifest anything I want, but I haven't had a great education and I'm stuck in an unfulfilling job with low pay. It's hard to see how I can really get ahead."*

Place your attention on finding the inner experience of success and prosperity, and let the outer world take care of itself. If you focus on your stuck place in the external world, you will remain stuck, whereas if you connect with your prosperity and success inwardly, your life will start to thrive outwardly, often in miraculous ways.

Love is Abundant

The irony is that you won't care so much, whether your outer life prospers or not. When you're completely fulfilled from within, you're not attached to a particular form of outer experience. It doesn't matter how much money you have, your level of education, or what your job is. It's possible for you to feel prosperous with any amount of money while doing any job.

Whatever your job may be, try to work from a consciousness of love. Give yourself in service and let your work be part of the whole. The Prophet, Kahlil Gibran writes, "When you work, you fulfill a part of Earth's furthest dream, assigned to you when that dream was born. And in keeping yourself with labor, you are in Truth loving life, and to love life through labor is to be intimate with life's inmost secret."

True work arises in a consciousness of love, not fear. When you love what you do with passion, performing your work with all your heart, your mental images stand out with clarity. Clear images, infused with the power of your enthusiasm, lead to the manifestation of what you want, to a life of prosperity. Think rich thoughts that recognize the abundance of the universe, and know that abundance is your divine inheritance.

Abundance is an aspect of your True Nature. It isn't something you obtain; it's an attribute of the love that you already are. Abundance is love and love is abundance. The consciousness of love therefore automatically attracts substance. You become like a magnet, drawing to you what is needed when it's needed. In a state of love, you do not have to grab what you want or manipulate others, any more than you have to make an effort to ensure that the Earth keeps orbiting the sun.

> *"So everyone is potentially abundant? What about the poor in Africa?"*

Don't get distracted by other people. Obviously, be considerate and caring, and help your fellow man. But don't use the predicaments of others as a reason to lose confidence in yourself. They have their own karma and destiny, which has been perfectly worked out for them, and you have yours. Focus on yourself, and change. By all means, help other people in need, but know that the biggest service you can give them is to transform yourself into your True Nature.

So claim your abundance now. Start by appreciating what you already have, even if you think it's far from perfect, and you'll find your experience of it begins to change for the better. Accept any situation you're in wholeheartedly, and watch what happens. You may be amazed at what transpires.

The Right Relationship with Money

Acceptance is a big key to your success. To accept what is, is to live a spiritual life. And spiritual living is prosperous living. When you align your thoughts with your True Self, you put yourself in the flow. And part of this flow is money; that's why we call it currency.

Know you can have all the money you want, but at the same time be perfectly happy about the amount of money you actually have. When you're in a right relationship with money, you have exactly the amount you need, whether it is a little or a lot, and you know it.

What is the correct relationship with money? It's to relinquish your ownership of it and to see it as it really is: a gift of love, to be used in service and sharing. Cultivate this attitude towards money and you will never experience another second of financial stress for the rest of your life.

Practice

1) Do your daily meditation.
2) At the end of your meditation period, begin your affirmation session. Set the intention of making the spiritual Truth contained in the affirmation change your experience of life.

TEXT 1- THE SETTING

Take a deep breath, relax, and align yourself with your breathing. Listen to your breath as it flows in and out of your body. Now visualize yourself entering a pyramid. This is your secret sanctuary, and it is filled with stillness and peace. You sit down on a beautiful throne that is the perfect design for you, and perfectly comfortable. The only energies in this pyramid are your own inner energies. You are completely protected from the external world.

TEXT 2 -THE INVOCATION

I invoke the energy of all the angels, archangels and masters. I call on the violet flame to consume, dissolve and purify all my dense thoughts and emotions. I ask for the release of any tendency to be attached, for my attachments are what inhibit the flow of love and separate me from the Light.

TEXT 3- THE AFFIRMATIONS

- I am a child of love, rich in Light, and always provided for.
- I am a master in all that I do.
- I deLight in giving to others, knowing that giving and receiving are the same.
- I appreciate what I have.
- Everything I touch prospers.
- I am melting the boundaries of my limited identity and merging with all of creation.
- I am a channel of divine Light and wisdom.
- I am the love that illumines the whole universe.
- I am the infinite love that attracts all substance to me, which brings forth my success.
- I am all abundance, all health, all wealth, all love, and all life.

Choose one of the above affirmations and repeat it as often as possible during the day. Set the intention of making the spiritual Truth contained in the affirmation change your experience of life.

Your Sacred Purpose

You cannot live without a purpose, and yet that is what you do when you are disconnected from the Light. A purpose gives meaning to life, and a meaningful life is what you're seeking. Without meaning, there is chaos, which makes you miserable and afraid. Meaning brings you joy.

Fortunately, you do have a purpose. Everyone, including you, has a function. Moreover, your part is essential to the Divine plan. (Yes, there is a plan; that's never been the issue. The only problem is that you haven't been aware of it.)

When you have a purpose, it means that your mind has been healed, made whole. You have become aware of the Wholeness that is your True Nature. You no longer see fragmented pieces, wrongly believing yourself to be separated and isolated. You see the unity that holds everything as one. A purpose is a unifying force because it makes you aware of your connection with the Source of Life and your part in fulfilling the Divine plan. When you're in touch with your purpose, your mind is quiet and your true mission is clear. Right ideas then flow through you.

Purpose and Identity

Most people have no real purpose and secretly perceive their lives as meaningless. This is because they identify with their body.

But bodies have no goal, and therefore your True Self cannot share its purpose with them. Only the Mind can share in your True purpose.

When you are identified with the body, you take actions solely for personal gain, such as doing a job just for the money. When you are identified with the Light, on the other hand, you do something just because it is the right thing to do. And out of your righteous action comes pure joy, because your selfless giving connects you with who you truly are, which is joy.

Therefore, to discover your purpose in life, you must first end the separation and discover who you are. Your belief in separation comes from perceiving things the wrong way around, which is wrong-mindedness. You have to get into your right mind and heal the mistaken identity that you are a body, which means to accept your true identity.

Put down your shield and sword and approach the Source of Truth without defenses. Truth is not dangerous; it's your only place of safety. Wake up from the dream and recognize who you are, what your purpose is, and what you have to do. Then you will know where you are going because finally you'll know who's in charge. You'll know that you are only the channel through which Life is pouring itself. You'll be able to relax because your True Self will be guiding you every step of the way.

Food nourishes your body and rest nourishes your mind, but true Love words nourish your soul. So what words are you allowing to proceed from your mouth-words of fragmentation or words of Wholeness? Let words of Wholeness proceed from you by quieting your mind so that you can hear your real thoughts.

Be still and know the Truth.

More on Discipline

It takes discipline to be still and listen. The word discipline means to learn, and so you have to open your mind to new learning that goes beyond everything that you have ever known intellectually. It takes great effort and willingness to do that. It's difficult because you want to oppose your true will, which is the same thing as opposing your peace and happiness. You continue to believe in your small will, without bothering to evaluate where it has taken you. Ask yourself, "Am I happy all the time in everything I do?" Unless you are, you are not following your true will.

> *"It seems unrealistic to be happy constantly. Just look at the world: you'd have to be blind to go about your life without a care in the world."*

According to your beliefs about reality, of course it isn't realistic to be continually joyful. Therefore, you have to question your beliefs deeply and sincerely. You have to be willing to learn something entirely new. Ask yourself, "Am I truly open to learning or am I heavily defended against learning? Have I built my home on a foundation of intellectual knowledge, and thus prevented myself from knowing the Truth? Perceiving the insecurity in everything I have created myself, have I then erected defenses in order to protect myself?" Drop your defenses, and then you will know what your purpose is and what you have to do. You'll become certain of your direction.

> *"Why do I have defenses in the first place?"*

Because you don't see yourself as you were created. You identify with a self-image that you've made up and mistakenly think is real. This image tells you that you are, "weak, vicious, ugly and sinful, miserable and beset with pain." Seeing yourself as lacking, limited, insecure, lonely, depressed, and deprived, you feel vulnerable and in need of protection. But you are misperceiving yourself. Your True Self does not see you that way. Heal the mistaken identity, and accept yourself as you were created. You have a choice: you can be fearful, resentful, and separate, or you can be loving, forgiving, and unifying. You can have a meaningless life or a meaningful life.

How do you see yourself? As loving, lovely, and lovable? Or, do you love yourself sometimes and hate yourself at other times? When you live in love more and more each day, you gradually shift your identification to your True Nature, which is love. You see the illusion of the world, but you no longer live in it. You live in the Truth, because your mind is healed.

When your mind is healed, it is at peace. Your energy is not scattered, but focused, because your attention is on what's at hand in the moment. You are aware of the body, but you realize that it is only part of your experience in this.

> *"Again, the usual question: How do I awaken from the dream?"*

Only by love is love awakened. And so in order to awaken the love within, you have to keep identifying with love. This takes mental discipline, constant awareness of what is going on within your mind. When a fearful thought enters, replace it with a loving thought. The more you discipline your mind to do this, the easier it will become, and it will not be long before you live continuously in a state of love.

> *"Haven't you said that we don't really know love? What does that mean?"*

Love does not exist in time, and therefore you do not truly know love because you still believe in time. Yet, time is an illusion existing only in your small mind. Therefore, to know love you have to transcend time and live in timelessness. Your body will still be subject to time—you'll drink, eat, walk, and talk—but, in your mind, you'll be aware that you are not limited by your body. You'll be connected to your purpose and function, and will live from your Wholeness. In your true nature, the divine plan is unfolding, and your part in it is clear. In this state of clarity, you are alive and inspired. To be inspired is to be in the spirit. If you're uninspired, you're not in the spirit—you are dispirited. When you are in the spirit, you are in love. When you're in love, you share, because sharing love is all you ever want to do when you're living from your True Nature. Form without spirit is useless. Intellectual knowledge, if it is not attached to spirit, is downright murderous, as all our wars demonstrate. The world's plans originate in confusion and therefore they can do nothing but generate more confusion. Therefore, let go of your plans and listen to your True Self's plan revealing itself to you in the quietness of your mind. All you have to do is listen and then step out in faith and perform the actions that are asked of you. You will not know the big picture, but you will know what must be done in the immediate future. To understand this, think of yourself traveling in a car at night. The headlights illuminate only a little section of the road, but that's enough. If you see the road ahead of you and the signs guiding you, then you can safely travel thousands of miles to distant cities.

The problem is that, on the road of life, there are pranksters erecting signs that give false directions. It takes constant awareness for you to distinguish the false signs from the genuine signs, and that's where discipline comes in. You have to distinguish between your ideas, which are leading you to misery, and divine ideas that will lead you to bliss. Notice the difference, and then choose the divine ideas that are seeking expression through you.

The Source of Certainty

You see, it's the Light, and not you, that's in command. You are only the channel. But what joy there is in being a conduit of love. As you open your mind to the energy of love, allowing it to flow, there is no confusion. You know exactly what to do. You are no longer dependent on the advice and opinions of other people. Your certainty comes from a place of infinite wisdom inside you.

> *"A state of certainty is a far cry from my present experience. I feel so indecisive all the time.*

That's because there is more than one of you making decisions. Many spiritual traditions teach that people are not the unified individuals they take themselves to be, and are in fact composed of multiple personalities. From this perspective, nearly everyone is suffering from Multiple Personality Disorder. (If you haven't been diagnosed as such, it means that you're able to integrate the personalities in a way that seems functional to the rest of society.) If you don't have a consistent identity, it's obviously impossible to know what action to take.

Although you're one Self, you experience yourself as two, as both good and evil, loving and hating, mind and body. This sense of being split into opposites induces feelings of acute and constant conflict. You keep oscillating between these opposites—between between fear and love—and that's why you're always in conflict. When you identify with the Light, the conflict ends because there is no conflict in Love and so there is none in you. Then decision-making becomes effortless.

Your Sacred Purpose

"*What is my purpose?*"

You have to discover it, which you can do by ending the conflict within you, which you do by waking up. Currently, you're asleep and dreaming that you're a body in a world of bodies. As a result, you see yourself as separate, isolated, and alienated. When you wake up, you live in the world of Love and know yourself to be whole. You see the unity that underlies all things. In this place of Wholeness, you have meaning and complete fulfillment. The purpose of your life becomes clear to you.

Your purpose is both universal and unique. It's universal because everyone's purpose is to be a pure expression of unconditional Love, and to participate in establishing love, joy, healing, wisdom, peace. It's also unique because your part in your True Self's plan requires the unique attributes of your soul, which were given to you when you were created. For this reason, the more deeply you immerse yourself in your sacred purpose, the more fully you become who you truly are.

When you understand how exquisite your True purpose is, you'll be astonished. You'll see that it is one of the most beautiful things in all of Creation.

Practice

1) Do your daily meditation.
2) At the end of your meditation period, begin your affirmation session.

TEXT 1 - THE SETTING

Take a deep breath, relax, and align yourself with your breathing. Listen to your breath as it flows in and out of your body. Now visualize yourself entering a pyramid. This is your secret sanctuary, and it is filled with stillness and peace. You sit down on a beautiful throne that is the perfect design for you, and perfectly comfortable. The only energies in this pyramid are your own inner energies. You are completely protected from the external world.

TEXT 2- THE INVOCATION

I invoke the energy of all the angels, archangels and masters. I call on the violet flame to consume, dissolve and purify all my dense thoughts and emotions. I ask for the release of any tendency to be attached, for my attachments are what inhibit the flow of love and separate me from the Light.

TEXT 3- THE AFFIRMATIONS

- My life is a glorious adventure.
- I place my talents into the hands of Love.
- I keep open the door of my mind and allow Truth to enter.
- I am shifting from separation to Wholeness, from fear to the remembrance of abundant Love consciousness.
- I am healing the distortion in my mind.
- I am allowing Love to heal my wounded emotional body.

- I am being amplified with love and grace.
- All that is dense is being shaken loose.
- All things that are being released from me are being released gradually and gracefully so that I may fulfill my divine purpose on Earth.
- My inner purpose is a deepening of what I am, the divinity within the divinity.
- I am leaving my imprint on the Earth to inspire and to encourage others to look within and discover a different approach to life, one that is fulfilling, purposeful, meaningful and offers peace.

Choose one of the above affirmations and repeat it as often as possible during the day. Set the intention of making the spiritual Truth contained in the affirmation change your experience of life.

The Power of Sharing

The physical world, if it is not interfered with by man, demonstrates that unconditional, unlimited sharing is its most fundamental law. The sun shines on you whether you're deserving or undeserving. Rain falls on you regardless of your gender or nationality. Whether you're rich or poor, old or young, saint or sinner, you get to hear the birdsong and smell the wildflowers. Whoever you are, the Earth keeps on hugging you to its surface, and it never checks to see if you've used up your allocation of gravity. The air continues circulating without regard to your gender, profession, or religion; indeed, a couple of the oxygen molecules you're inhaling right now might have previously been exhaled by Buddha or Jesus Christ.

This principle of unconditional sharing also holds true in the invisible world of Spirit. Like air, Light, and water, Love shares itself endlessly, without limitation. You don't have to work for it or create it; you only have to allow it. Sharing is the essence of love, and so when you share love, you are love. This is why the wise devote themselves selflessly to the welfare of the world, whereas the ignorant focus on their personal wellbeing. You can experience nothing more fulfilling and rewarding than sharing love unconditionally, because there's nothing more fulfilling and rewarding than being you.

The Law of Multiplication

If you want there to be more love in the world and in your life, you need to begin by giving love to others. If you approach life from the perspective of the small mind, which tells you that there's not enough of anything to go around, not even love, then you will create a world around you that is lacking in love. But if you share love with others, you'll begin to create a world around you that is filled with people sharing love. Therefore, sharing is an extraordinarily powerful tool in your spiritual toolbox.

You don't have to do anything to share love; the sharing happens simply by your being who you are. When you're identified with the Light, your nature is to share. All sharing is equally valuable. If you're standing in front of a television camera, addressing a billion people, or sitting on your own in a park, your inner Light radiates the same love in the same way, and it transforms the world. Only your unnatural mind sees one situation as more important than another. Your natural mind doesn't experience these distinctions, because its love is whole and undifferentiated.

> *"Don't we have to be realistic? I mean, everyone else, pretty much, is out to get what they can for themselves. So don't I need to do the same thing too? If I just share and share endlessly, won't the world simply walk all over me?"*

There is nothing to get. You already have and are everything. Therefore, getting is meaningless, whereas giving is an expression of your True Nature. Moreover, since you receive what you give, your choice about what to give is also your choice about what you receive. Offer your brother thorns and you are crucified. Offer him lilies and it is yourself you free. The crucified give pain because they are in pain. The free give love because they are love.

Do not confuse pain with joy, or fear with love. When you are angry, hateful, resentful, or condemning, you are in pain and fear. If you insist on holding onto these feelings, it's because you unconsciously imagine that they will ultimately lead to the joy and love that are your true goals. They won't. Fear and pain merely reproduce themselves endlessly. When you're afraid, you share your fear with others, and they share it with others, and so on. The fear grows exponentially and as a result we live in a fearful world.

Returning Home

You can change your fear-based life, but it's a gut-wrenching task because it means that you have to let go of the thought system that you have invested in so heavily. Your small self tries to fill itself up from the outside, and yet it can never succeed in doing this. Your True Self, on the other hand, is filled from inside, and so it can always share itself because its source is never depleted. When you're living from the Light, you share your fullness because you already have everything, and so you don't want anything back from the other person. All you want to do is share your love.

Through daily practice, you can let go of your ego-based thoughts and accept your real thoughts that are within you but which are presently covered up. These beliefs are harming you, but you're so identified with them that you're blind to them. Nevertheless, there comes a time when you begin to suspect that what your physical eyes are showing you is not real. You look around you and say, "This is not home." And then you ask the question that will begin to change your life, "Where is home? If it can't be here, so where is it?"

"And the answer to that question is?"

Your home is your True Nature, your natural mind, the part of you that shares pure love with others. When you give up your fake love, you return home, and then genuine love shines from you like a beacon.

Love and Sharing

> *"I feel uncomfortable about the implication that none of my love is genuine. If it's not real then what is it?"*

We're not saying that your never experienced unconditional love. If you have children, you may well have given them selfless love on many occasions. However, as discussed in Chapter 8, in most of your relationships, your love is a kind of barter, in which you say to the other person (without realizing it), "For as long as you behave in ways that make me feel good, and thus create a context in which I am able to experience love, I will continue to direct love towards you." This is a form of relationship, in which you perceive differences rather than Wholeness. The other person has something you want and you're in the relationship to get it from him or her. When there's nothing left to take, you move on to the next relationship. But wherever you go you bring your thoughts with you, and so unless you correct the fundamental error (the perception of differences), you will find it rearing its ugly head again and again. As a result, despite your best efforts to find true intimacy with the next person, your baggage of likes, dislikes, habits, opinions, attachments, and prejudices will inevitably create distance between you and the other instead of the closeness for which you yearn. When you give up this facsimile of love, you allow true Love to take up residence within you. And what a joy that is. There is no longer any compulsion to take, get, grab, compete for, acquire or achieve anything. You are as you were created. You are love. You are whole and undivided. You don't need anything because you are everything. True intimacy is now possible since you and the other are no longer separate. In this state of Wholeness, you are overflowing with love and goodness. You are so inconceivably full of blessings that you can't stop them spilling out onto others. Your Light illuminates the entire world so that wherever your gaze rests, you see everything and everyone as inexpressibly whole. This is the bliss of sharing.

"Doesn't it take two to share? I mean, don't I need the other person's cooperation to share true love with them?"

Don't wait for another person to do the work, or else you'll be waiting forever. Fortunately, you have much more power to influence the other person than you imagine. You have no influence when you employ the ego's tactics of control and manipulation; they just generate more resistance. But when you perceive the situation as an opportunity to heal both yourself and the other person, you change it. By releasing him from every demand your ego would make of him, you heal him by showing him that his illusions are not true. At the same time, you break down your own illusions and heal yourself. The mind we share is shared by all our brothers, and as we see them truly they will be healed. That, in a nutshell, is the power of sharing.

When you share love with another person, which means to see him truly, you give him a blessing that you need just as much as he does. You receive this blessing by giving it. When you see the Light in another person, you become aware of the Light inside you. Conversely, when you deny another person's Light, which you do when you judge him, you deny your own Light. In other words, you see Light in everybody or you see it in nobody, including yourself, because Light is Wholeness and you cannot see Wholeness and separation at the same time. For this reason, the way you see another person is the way you see yourself, and therefore the other person is a mirror image of you. Do not deny a brother his blessing. To deny his blessing means that you judge him and thus reinforce the Grand Illusion. When you do this, you keep him in a prison, and you keep yourself in the same prison right alongside him. Your forgiveness, which means to see past the illusion into the other person's True Nature, releases you both.

When you begin to glimpse the perfection of this mechanism and start to use it for your own benefit, the transformation of your life begins in earnest.

So, make it your firm intention every day to act from love and not from fear, and then watch yourself as you go about your daily business. As often as you can, catch yourself trying to get things from other people and from life in general, and switch your perspective. Ask yourself, "What would love do now?" You'll be surprised at how eager love is to answer that question when you ask it. "How would love act in this situation?" Follow the direction that is given to you, and you'll discover the exquisite joy of sharing love unconditionally with other people. You'll no longer have to manipulate them so that they change; they'll automatically change because everyone and everything is transformed by love.

When my children were little, we were sitting on the curb outside our house with the other kids in the neighborhood. One of the neighbor's dogs came down the street, and my daughter said, "Mom, that dog is so mean. He barks at us and we all have to run away." And sure enough, the dog began to bark, and the children started to run away. The kids were all looking back at me expecting me to run, but I just sat there. The children were worried, but I wanted them to see that we're all connected to one another, even to the drooling, barking dog that was approaching us. I wanted to demonstrate to them that if we are able to let go of fear, and radiate nothing but pure love, what is fearful cannot help but become loving too. And when the dog reached me, it stopped barking and allowed me to stroke it. It was a beautiful moment.

> *"I want to radiate love all the time, but I'm not sure I really can tell the difference between false and genuine love."*

Life will show you every time: wait a while, and watch what happens when the person stops behaving as you wish. If your love is conditional, it will turn to hate, in which case it was not love. Also, if you pay attention to what's going on inside you, you will see that underneath conditional love there is a feeling of tension, because when you are unconsciously bartering with another person, you are always secretly afraid that you will not get what you want. The basic concept of a trade is that you don't have something that you think you need. If you give love to another person in exchange for prescribed behaviors, you are effectively stating to yourself that you only possess love in certain circumstances, while in other situations you lack love. This is why conditional love is fueled by fear.

The dark belief that you fundamentally lack love (and thus are dependent on the outside world for any love that you experience), creates the Hell that you live in. The more you operate in the world of conditional love-the trade-the more you experience a fundamental lack of love. The more you experience lack of love, the more you attempt to grab it, and the more you grab it the more it eludes you. The antidote to this vicious circle is to practice sharing love unconditionally, which means giving love even when you don't feel like it. This is going to be a big job. Every time you see something or someone, your instinctive reaction is to slip into judgment. This is not love, because judgment and genuine love cannot coexist any more than midday and midnight can. But judging has become such a "normal" part of your experience that you don't realize you're doing it, especially with people close to you who are triggering your deepest wounds.

Therefore, it's wise to start simply, choosing love instead of judgment in relatively undemanding situations. When people cut you off on the freeway, or push a full shopping cart into the express line in the supermarket (and refuse to let you and your one carton of milk go ahead of them), or criticize your work and call you a fool, just smile at them. You might have to force the smile at first, but since it's difficult to smile and be judgmental at the same time, your smile will become increasingly authentic.

You and the Others

When you allow your sharing nature to surface more and more, you start to see the Truth about judgment: you're only judging yourself. You are the other person and the other person is you. What you see in him, you see in yourself. What you think of him, you think of yourself. What you do to him, you do to yourself. In a real sense, there's no one out there but you.

These are not abstract concepts; they are real. Suppose that somebody you're interacting with annoys you because they are hogging the limelight. You think, "All he ever talks about is himself; he hasn't asked a single question about anybody else's life—especially mine!" Look at the situation dispassionately and you'll realize that it is you who wants the limelight; if you could hog it yourself, you'd do exactly that. It doesn't matter if you are the most timid person on earth, who has never once been the life and soul of the party, you nevertheless secretly hanker for attention. Therefore, the individual that you are judging in this example is in fact mirroring a quality that you dislike in yourself. You tell yourself that it's a form of behavior that you dislike in others, which is why you don't do it yourself; but the Truth is that it's a behavior that you secretly desire for yourself but have been repressing. Seen in this Light, your judgment of the other person is a self-judgment.

If you were not judging yourself, the other person's behavior would not create a change in you. You would still observe that this person likes to be the center of attention, but you would no longer react to it with emotional upset. You would remain clear and present and you would be receptive to the guidance of unconditional love, which would show you how to act. This may be something no more spectacular than moving to another part of the room; but sometimes love, speaking through you, might say a few words to this person, or take a simple action, that will cause his life to go in an entirely different direction from that point forth. Whenever you share unconditional love, which is entirely free of judgment, you will act in a way that serves the highest good of others and thus serves your highest good.

Above the Fog

> *"That sounds simple, and yet it seems so hard to put into practice."*

You find it hard because your mind is so untrained and undisciplined. You go through the motions, appearing to act out of love, but in fact, you keep reacting out of fear. You don't know how to act out of love because you have never been trained. From the time you were little, you have been conditioned by your environment, which has dictated to you your likes and dislikes and all your opinions. The environment consisted first of your parents and their belief system, which they shared with you. They didn't know any better; they were only sharing what they felt was right. Next, this set of beliefs was reinforced and amplified by teachers, ministers, politicians, entertainers, friends, and so on. By the time you entered adulthood, you had become lost in a fog of beliefs, so much so that you stopped even noticing the fog.

If you're fortunate enough to come from a city with clean air, and you fly to Los Angeles in the summer, you will see a striking analogy of this. As you pass over the city, you look down upon thick, brown smog and you wonder how anybody could live in those conditions. Once you've landed and are walking around downtown or Disneyland, or wherever your destination is, you discover to your astonishment that the local residents think nothing of the health hazards that they live with daily. In fact, they don't even notice the problem anymore. You can't imagine how they could be so insensitive. But after a few days, you become acclimatized; your eyes stop watering, your lungs don't hurt any more, and you no longer see that you're walking through a toxic haze. If a newly arrived stranger complained about the situation, you might not immediately understand what he was talking about. Similarly, you've become used to your smoggy thoughts and don't notice them anymore. When you rise above them, however, you can see them again, and you realize that they're not your true home. Your thoughts are hooked into outer places and conditions, but your home is inside you. So, that's where you need to have the discipline to look. You have to confirm what can only be confirmed by you, that your true home is within you. You have to realize that the beliefs you've held onto since childhood, which have dictated your identity to you, are false. When you understand what you are not, the Truth of what you are can then be revealed to you. And the Truth is that you are pure and whole. When you know yourself, you see everything as whole and undivided. You see with eyes of love.

Enlightened Self-Interest

> *"What about the really painful situations to do with family or friends? It seems such a leap to love a person who has betrayed and abused you. How do you keep on sharing love in those circumstances?"*

You have to remember who's benefiting from your sharing: You are. Sharing love with someone who appears to have harmed you might seem like "letting them off the hook" when they don't deserve it, but it's also letting you off the hook. So if you can think of no other reason to share unconditional love with another, do it for reasons of self-interest. There's nothing wrong with enlightened self-interest; it causes you to seek happiness and fulfillment where it can be found, rather than where it can't be found. When you're confronted with difficult people and painful situations, you welcome them enthusiastically because you know that they're offering you a gift that you want. They're showing you the places inside you that need to receive the healing balm of your unconditional love. The person or situation has been given to you to help you grow. Belief in enemies is the belief in weakness, which is a belief in the unreal. The Truth is that there are no enemies, only friends; no weakness, only strength.

It's hard to remember that life is consistently helping you. Very powerful conditioning pushes you to look outside yourself and make people and events responsible for what you experience. The whole world seems obsessed with blaming others, so much so that you seem abnormal if you don't conform. (Try being consistently unconcerned about anything that happens to you in your finances, your relationships, your workplace, or any other area of your life:

The people close to you will probably worry that you've become mentally ill.)

It requires a great deal of determination to go against the tide of deluded human thinking. I once received a phone call from a student who was complaining about his ex-girlfriend. Not only had she run off with another man, but to add insult to injury she'd also taken Lulu, the dog, which, my student told me—in vehement tones—belonged to him. The woman then had the gall to ask my student to let her back into the house so that she could collect some of the dog's belongings. The poor man became almost apoplectic as he recited this catalog of horrors to me. I said, "Well, you know from everything you've learned that it's not the other person. She is just the mirror that's reflecting your own lack of self-love and your own betrayal." My student was indignant, "I'm not going to let her back into the house. I'll call the police if she tries to get in. I'll get a restraining order. I can prove that Lulu is mine." I interrupted him: "Hold it, hold it. You know what? You're attacking. Why don't you choose love instead of attack? Instead of saying you're not going to do this for her, why don't you act out of love and do it anyway?" "I'm not going to give her that satisfaction", he replied. You're not doing it for her satisfaction," I said, "You're doing it for yourself."

While you're stuck in the illusory world of the small mind, a situation like this can be excruciatingly painful. In some instances, it can even lead to murder; so, the intensity of the pain is not to be underestimated. Nevertheless, however strong the feelings may be, they are being triggered by an illusion. It isn't true that you've been betrayed and hurt. Why? Because it isn't true that you're separate from your ex-girlfriend, the dog and the other man. Who you truly are can never lose anything. The sooner you learn this, the sooner you can move into a life where this kind of thing doesn't keep happening.

The Jewel in the Pain

"How do I learn this?"

You learn by doing it. You observe yourself going into a pattern of judgment, resentment, envy, or whatever else, and you choose to share love instead. You may not know what the actions of unconditional love will look like, but if you invoke love into the situation, it will come and it will show you what to do and say. You may not master the process perfectly at first, but with practice, you will get better at it, and then your life will get better. You will see the True Nature in everyone and you will experience much less struggle. Perhaps you think, "My treacherous ex-lover's True Nature is too remote to be perceived right now, if indeed it exists at all." Well, if you can't perceive the Light within him, you can perceive your own feelings, and so that's where you need to start. Exercise enough willpower to withdraw your attention from what's going on outside you so that you can go inwards and examine your pain. Inside your pain, you will find a jewel. If you do not repress the pain or distract yourself from it, it will reveal to you a wounded part of your psyche. The awareness you bring to this wound is unconditional love, and love heals. Therefore, staying present with your pain will free you from it. You don't have to figure out why the pain is there, or determine its origin, or discover a cure. The healing is done automatically, without your conscious help. The rewards of making a breakthrough with this or any other painful situation are enormous. The reason is that you see yourself as you see others, and so if you see them as flawed or downright evil, you also see yourself as flawed or evil. Real, unconditional sharing clears your perception so that you can gradually see the other person's True Nature, and thus become aware of your own True Nature.

Your True Nature is love and the other person's nature is love too; when you find yourself face to face with Love, everything vanishes but Love. This is why sharing is such a powerful catalyst for your spiritual growth.

Another Look at Forgiveness

> *"Don't I have to do some forgiveness work with the really difficult people in my life before I see the Light in them?"*

Yes, but remember that the forgiveness is about you, not the other person. Lack of forgiveness is a poison, and you are the one who has swallowed it. The unforgiving mind sees only fear and is in despair, for it believes that the ills it sees cannot be remedied. Forgiveness lets you recognize the Truth and allows the wisdom to enter your mind. Therefore, forgiveness releases you from the fear of your own making. Remember also that what you're forgiving is an illusion, which your forgiveness causes to disappear. When you forgive, you are releasing yourself and others from the illusion. Your forgiveness literally transforms your vision and lets you see the real world bringing you into the present.

You've been dreaming that there are other people in the world who've harmed you. That's all it's been: a dream. When you wake up from a nightmare, do you approach the actors in the dream and forgive them for what they did? No, the need for forgiveness vanishes along with the dream.

> *"So what do I do about the people in my life who I feel I need to forgive?"*

Don't do anything. True forgiveness requires no visible action, for it is an inner correction in the mind, in which you drop all judgments and shift into a state of total acceptance. Dropping all judgments doesn't mean that you suddenly decide that everything you experience is good. It means that you realize that you don't know the true meaning of anything that happens. Therefore, forgiveness is the suspension of judgment, which clears the mind of your mistaken beliefs and leaves room for love to enter. When in love, a miracle seems to occur: nothing is what you thought it was; everything is perfect exactly the way it is.

The other person is no longer the source of your pain, but the agent of your deliverance. He is an emissary of the Light, placed on the planet to help you heal. And in this instant of recognition, you finally know yourself. You are an emissary of the Light too, born to share love and healing with your fellow man.

Practice

1) Do your daily meditation.
2) At the end of your meditation period, begin your affirmation session.

TEXT 1 - THE SETTING

Take a deep breath, relax, and align yourself with your breathing. Listen to your breath as it flows in and out of your body. Now visualize yourself entering a pyramid. This is your secret sanctuary, and it is filled with stillness and peace. You sit down on a beautiful throne that is the perfect design for you, and perfectly comfortable. The only energies in this pyramid are your own inner energies. You are completely protected from the external world.

TEXT 2 -THE INVOCATION

I invoke the energy of all the angels, archangels and masters. I call on the violet flame to consume, dissolve and purify all my dense thoughts and emotions. I ask for the release of any tendency to be, attached, for my attachments are what inhibit the flow of love and separate me from the Light.

TEXT 3- THE AFFIRMATIONS

- I practice unconditional sharing by inviting spiritual law to govern my life.
- I love my neighbor as myself.

- I seek first to know my true self, knowing that all else will be added to me.
- I do unto others as I would have them do unto me.
- I ask, knowing that I shall receive.
- I do not live by bread alone but by every word that proceeds from my mouth.
- I am what I think in my heart.
- By faith am I made whole.
- I reap what I sow.
- By obeying spiritual law, I connect with the Light of my True Self and perfect outcomes—for others as well as for myself—come into manifestation.

The Innocent Mind

When you dissolve your self-created mind and allow the Light inside you to emerge, you discover that who you are is wholly innocent. Innocence is the natural state of the mind, in which you know you are one with life. It's a state of faith that arises spontaneously when you stop depending on the outer world and instead recognize that your security comes from the Innocent Mind, not man-made rules and ideas.

The Innocent Mind is True

The innocent mind lives in the Truth, and does not fear it or interfere with it. Being unacquainted with evil, innocence is free from guilt or sin. It is wise, trusting, and strong. It doesn't blame or condemn, nor does it ever misperceive situations or people. It always sees truly, with single vision, and that is the origin of its unassailable strength.

The Innocent Mind is Humble

Innocence is an attribute of humility. To be humble is to deny all external influences, recognizing that you are dependent only on the Source of Life. The arrogant cling to words because they are afraid to transcend them, whereas the innocent mind abides in a world beyond words, a world of gentleness and patience that asserts itself meekly.

"Blessed are the meek: for they shall inherit the Earth" (Matthew 5:5-10 KJV), because their perception is clear. In the man-made world of illusions, we see meekness as weakness, but the opposite is true. Your clarity of vision—achievable only in a state of egoless humility—gives you the greatest possible protection, which is the removal of any need for protection. Therefore, always look within with meekness, humility, and love. Take pride in being humble!

The Innocent Mind is Pure

The innocent mind is pure, whole and free. Your self-created thoughts form a fog that blocks your perception of your innocence. But the instant you let go of your mistaken beliefs, which are essentially a defense against reality, your innocent mind reappears, and you realize that everything is, always has been, and always will be, perfect.

The Innocent Mind is Guiltless

The Latin root of "innocence" signifies "to be unharmed". The opposite of innocence is "guilt", a word that has had a great deal of notoriety over the course of human history. In most countries, guilt is so pervasive in the culture that it mixes into a person's psyche almost from the womb and then is reinforced by the indoctrination received from the family, church, and school. No wonder so many people are triggered in so many ways by the word "guilt".

Some branches of Christianity speak of original sin, implying that humans are basically bad and need to improve themselves in order to be worthy of the Kingdom of Heaven. Some people embrace this doctrine enthusiastically, while others find it repugnant. The argument is raging within the illusion, and is therefore, itself part of the illusion, and thus meaningless. Humanity has not fallen from grace, but it has fallen asleep and is dreaming that it lives in a world in which it is disconnected from the Light, from its Source. When you wake up, you discover to your deLight that you are, and always have been, an inseparable part of the Light. If guilt is to do with xiling yourself from your true reality, then you have clearly never been guilty; you have always been innocent, and you always will be. When you wake up from a dream in which you've been harmed, where does the harm go? It cannot be absolved or pardoned, because it never happened.

If you make your own decisions about what you need in your life, you're assuming that you are alone and unsupported, which means you think you've been harmed, since your attitude supposes that you have become separated from the Source of Life. On the other hand, when you ask the Light to decide for you, you're in essence accepting your eternal innocence. You did not make your innocence; it was given to you and therefore your denial of what you are is arrogant. Lay aside your arrogance, which tells you that you are guilty and ashamed and lift up your heart in true humility. Now is the time to accept and appreciate who you are which is eternally powerful, loving, and whole. Exchange guilt for innocence by allowing your mind to reach inward to the wisdom that dwells within you. Guilt is a sure sign your thinking is unnatural. The ego's method of freeing you from guilt is to suppress it or project it. The Light's method is to be present. Come into the Light right now, and replace judgment with discernment, for judgment keeps you glued to the world of form, whereas discernment returns you to your inner Light, your innocence.

Return to the Innocent Mind

Reclaim your innocence, which is your True Nature, by letting go of your sticky, limiting thoughts and allowing your separate mind to dissolve. You do this by bringing your self-created beliefs up into the warmth of your awareness, so they may dissolve like ice-cubes in the sun.

Wake up, and know yourself. Return home now, to the Light within you. And from this point forth in your life, follow your own star.

Practice

1) Do your daily meditation.
2) At the end of your meditation period, begin your affirmation session.

TEXT 1 -THE SETTING

Take a deep breath, relax, and align yourself with your breathing. Listen to your breath as it flows in and out of your body. Now visualize yourself entering a pyramid. This is your secret sanctuary, and it is filled with stillness and peace. You sit down on a beautiful throne that is the perfect design for you, and perfectly comfortable. The only energies in this pyramid are your own inner energies. You are completely protected from the external world.

TEXT 2- THE INVOCATION

I call on the violet flame to consume, dissolve and purify all my dense thoughts and emotions. I ask for the release of any tendency to be attached, for my attachments are what inhibit the flow of love and separate me from the Light.

TEXT 3- THE AFFIRMATIONS

- I am an innocent child of the mighty "I AM" presence.
- I call on the mighty "I AM" presence to charge my entire mind, emotions, and body with the consciousness of the divine.
- Mighty "I AM" presence, bring the cosmic flame into my thoughts, emotions, body, and world, and wipe out all else.
- Mighty "I AM" presence, take from me every single feeling that obstructs me, so that my intelligent energy may go forth and produce the perfect result I desire.
- Mighty "I AM" presence, charge me so full of divine love that every person, place, and condition that I contact becomes instantly harmonious and obedient to the will of love.

- Mighty "I AM" presence, fill me with divine love, power, and perfect intelligent direction.
- Mighty "I AM" presence, consume in me and my world, all doubt, fear, jealousy, pride, resentment, irritation, criticism, condemnation, and judgment. Erase their cause, effect, and memory, and replace them with your Love.
- Mighty "I AM" presence, prepare my path and show me where to go, what to say, and what to do.
- Mighty "I AM" presence let me inwardly feel your Wholeness.
- I breathe the Divine Light. The Divine Light descends on me and purifies and blesses me.
- I rest in the unending peace of Eternal Light. I reclaim my innocence now and move forward in my life with lightened footsteps.

Appendix

Affirmations - The Complete Text

TEXT 1 -THE SETTING

Take a deep breath, relax, and align yourself with your breathing. Listen to your breath as it flows in and out of your body. Now visualize yourself entering a pyramid. This is your secret sanctuary, and it is filled with stillness and peace. You sit down on a beautiful throne that is the perfect design for you, and perfectly comfortable. The only energies in this pyramid are your own inner energies. You are completely protected from the external world.

TEXT 2 - THE INVOCATION

I invoke the energy of all the angels, archangels and masters. I call on the violet flame to consume, dissolve and purify all my dense thoughts and emotions. I ask for the release of any tendency to be attached, for my attachments are what inhibit the flow of love and separate me from the Light.

TEXT 3 - THE AFFIRMATIONS

Chapter 1—Unglue the Mind

- I unglue the Mind by releasing all judgments.
- I unglue the Mind by erasing my mental chalkboard and starting with a clean slate.
- I unglue the Mind by allowing myself simply to be.

- I unglue the Mind by unwinding the illusion that has surrounded me and remembering to be one with my True Nature, my "I AM" presence.
- I unglue the Mind by learning to live completely in the present, where every moment is the best, where every experience is new, fresh and alive.
- I unglue the Mind by freeing myself from the prison of the past with its haunting memories and vain regrets, and freeing myself from the prison of the future with its tantalizing hopes and tormenting fears.
- I unglue the Mind by letting go of doubt and fear and allowing the certainty and love of my natural mind to arise.
- All of the enormous energy formerly trapped in the past and the future flows to me here and now. I am using this energy to alleviate the suffering of those around me.
- In living for others, I come alive.
- I am being lifted up to a state of awareness.
- I sail through life with ease and grace, eager to serve my mighty "I AM" presence.

Chapter 2— Your Natural Mind

- I am returning to my natural state, where my mind operates from my Higher Self.
- I release all of my creations that separate me from the Light.
- Everything in my life that is bitter is becoming sweet.
- I am reuniting with my Light body, melting the boundaries of my limited identity and merging with all of creation.
- I am releasing all useless pursuits and idle thoughts. Thoughts have no substance; I allow them to arise and pass away.
- I am holding my mind in silent readiness to receive the gift of love.
- Every cell of my body is vibrant and filled with divine Light.
- In the quiet of my natural Mind, constant guiding thoughts are whispered to my soul.

Chapter 3— Your True Nature

- I rest in the loving arms of my True Nature, which is one with God.
- Everything I need is present within me.
- I am safe because I am whole.
- I am invulnerable and eternal.
- I enjoy the outside world because I do not depend on it.
- I dwell within my True Nature and I see beauty in all things.
- I live from my True Nature, which is the source of my power, contentment, and peace.

Chapter 4—Choose the Light

- I choose the Light.
- I am releasing all that I've been holding onto for security and satisfaction.
- Regardless of my perception, I know that I am being transformed and that all is well.
- I am gentle with myself. I accept myself and I am kind to myself.
- I am content in every moment.
- I am reuniting with my Light body and with the awareness that I have lost.
- I perform every task with a grateful attitude, thankful that I can be used.
- The channel is open and I put myself in the service of the Light.

Chapter 5—Walking the Path of Gratitude

- I am grateful for this day; whatever transpires I face with love and understanding.
- I perform every task with a grateful attitude, thankful that I can be used, that the channel is open and I can be of service.
- I am grateful that the Light in me awakens the Light in all.
- I am grateful my mind is absolutely committed to everything that is real.

- I am grateful that I'm willing to create a future unlike the past.
- I am grateful that nothing external to me can hurt or injure me.
- I am grateful that everything is already decided for me by my True Self.
- I am grateful for the priceless gift of spiritual awareness.
- I am grateful that the path I walk in life leads only to the Light.
- I am grateful I know no law except the law of love.
- I am grateful I am the Light that illumines the entire universe.

Chapter 6— Harnessing the Sacred Power of Stillness

- I am calm, quite, confident and assured.
- I am released from conflict.
- I am drinking from the waters of peace.
- All that is weak is being burnt away.
- I see all things in terms of love.
- I ask for complete and total protection to see my True Self, my "I AM" presence.
- All of my thoughts are purified.
- I recognize the universal force behind the world, the invisible power that flows through matter.
- All that is not of Light is melting away, like mist in the sun. Nothing happens without my consent.
- I am responsible for my thoughts.
- I am liberating myself from slavery.
- My life is no longer regulated by anything external.
- I love myself unconditionally.
- I am listening in the silence.
- I am listening with my heart.

Chapter 7— Love

- I am encircled in the protective presence of love.
- I am an unstoppable force of love.

- I am taking a bath in a pool of love.
- I am pouring upon my body temple the oil of love.
- I am radiating love in all directions endlessly.
- I am giving myself the gift of love.
- I am on a path of love, joy, and peace.
- I am showered with love and blessings.
- I am breathing in love and breathing out love.
- I am giving and receiving love freely, for I am love.

Chapter 8 — Enlightened Relationships

- I see the Light in the eyes of everyone I meet and recognize them as I see myself.
- I see a teacher in everyone I meet, and I strive to learn the lesson. I see myself without seeking to give the other person a lesson.
- Each day, my relationships are becoming more peaceful, more loving, and more fun.
- I discover my enlightened Self by seeing the enlightened Self in others.
- I accept myself and my life unconditionally.
- I am melting the boundaries of my limited identity and merging with all of creation.
- I am holding my mind in silent readiness to receive the gift of love.

Chapter 9—The Perception of Truth

- I am polishing the mirror of my mind each day.
- I am feasting on the Truth.
- My True Self sees all things as pure.
- I see the current of life flowing behind all forms.
- I see my reflection in everyone.
- My worth is established by my True Self.
- I am here to experience the deliciousness of life by removing everything that blocks my perception of love.

- I experience the bliss and satisfaction that comes from my union with the divine.
- I am healing the ills of my mind with the medicine of Truth.
- I am overflowing with gratitude to be in physical form in this moment in time.
- I am experiencing more of what I am and less of what I've made.
- I am a pulsating being of Light, radiating through the body.
- I am keeping my fire burning through daily practice.
- My humble efforts are fruitful.
- I am letting go of my limited desires and my limited existence.

Chapter 10— Making your True Self's Thoughts Yours

- I surrender my thoughts to my True Self.
- I rest in my True Self's thoughts.
- I am floating in the river of life, easily and gracefully.
- I am partaking of the mystical joys of life.
- The Light descends on me and I am purified and blessed. I am filled with a sense of my original identity.
- I breathe the divine breath.
- I am living in my natural environment.
- My inner faculties are developed and expanding.
- I am living and working with supreme confidence.
- My gentle approach to life is my strength.
- I am drinking at the fountain of wisdom.
- I am giving the highest expression of myself in everything I undertake.
- I am the knowing principle in all things.

Chapter 11—Effortless Prosperity

- I am a child of Love, rich in spirit, and always provided for.
- I am a Master in all that I do.
- I delight in giving to others, knowing that giving and receiving are the same.
- I appreciate what I have.

- Everything I touch prospers.
- I am melting the boundaries of my limited identity and merging with all of creation.
- I am a channel of Light and Wisdom.
- I am the love that illumines the whole universe.
- I am the infinite love that attracts all substance to me, which brings forth my success.
- I am all abundance, all health, all wealth, all love, and all life.

Chapter 12— Your Sacred Purpose

- My life is a glorious adventure.
- I place my talents into the hands of love.
- I keep open the door of my mind and allow Truth to enter.
- I am shifting from separation to Wholeness, from fear to the remembrance of abundant love consciousness.
- I am healing the distortion in my mind.
- I am allowing love to heal my wounded emotional body.
- I am being amplified with love and grace.
- All that is dense is being shaken loose.
- All things that are being released from me are being released gradually and gracefully so that I may fulfill my divine purpose on Earth.
- My inner purpose is a deepening of what I am, the divinity within the divinity.
- I am leaving my imprint on the Earth to inspire and to encourage others to look within and discover a different approach to life, one that is fulfilling, purposeful, meaningful and offers peace.

Chapter 13— The Power of Sharing

- I practice unconditional sharing by inviting spiritual law to govern my life.
- I love my neighbor as myself.
- I seek first to know my true self, knowing that all else will be added to me.

- I do unto others as I would have them do unto me.
- I ask, knowing that I shall receive.
- I do not live by bread alone but by every word that proceeds from my mouth.
- I am what I think in my heart.
- By faith am I made whole.
- I reap what I sow.
- By obeying spiritual law, I connect with my True Self's energy, and perfect outcomes—for others as well as for myself—come into manifestation.

Chapter 14—The Innocent Mind

- I am an innocent child of the mighty "I AM" presence that is my True Self.
- I call on the mighty "I AM" presence to charge my entire mind, emotions, and body with the consciousness of Love.
- Mighty "I AM" presence, bring the cosmic flame into my thoughts, emotions, body, and world, and wipe out all else.
- Mighty "I AM" presence, take from me every single feeling that obstructs me, so that my intelligent energy may go forth and produce the perfect result.
- Mighty "I AM" presence, charge me so full of divine love that every person, place, and condition that I contact becomes instantly harmonious and obedient to the will of love.
- Mighty "I AM" presence, fill me with love, power, and perfect intelligent direction.
- Mighty "I AM" presence, consume in me and my world all doubt, fear, jealousy, pride, resentment, irritation, criticism, condemnation and judgment. Erase their cause, effect, and memory and replace them with Love.
- Mighty "I AM" presence, prepare my path and show me where to go, what to say, and what to do.

- Mighty "I AM" presence, let me inwardly feel your Wholeness. I breathe the divine Light.
- The divine Light descends on me and purifies and blesses me.
- I rest in the unending peace of Eternal Light. I reclaim my innocence.

Printed and bound by PG in the USA